TAGMEMICS, DISCOURSE,
and
VERBAL ART

TAGMEMICS, DISCOURSE, AND VERBAL ART

Kenneth L. Pike
Professor Emeritus
The University of Michigan

Edited and with a Preface by
Richard W. Bailey

ANN ARBOR
Michigan Studies in the Humanities
1981

© 1981 by the University of Michigan

Michigan Studies in the Humanities
Horace H. Rackham School of Graduate Studies

Board of Editors

Richard Bailey (English), Judith Becker (Music), Arthur Burks (Philosophy), Oscar Büdel (Italian), Vern Carroll (Anthropology), Herbert Eagle (Film), Emery George (German), Floyd Gray (French), D. Kirkpatrick (History of Art), Ladislav Matejka (Slavic), Walter Mignolo (Spanish), Eric Rabkin (American Studies), G. Rosenwald (Psychology), Ingo Seidler (German), Gernot Windfuhr (Near Eastern Studies).

Irwin R. Titunik, *Associate Editor*
Ladislav Matejka, *Managing Editor*

Library of Congress Cataloging in Publication Data

Pike, Kenneth Lee, 1912-
 Tagmemics, discourse, and verbal art.

 (Michigan studies in the humanities; no. 3)
 1. Tagmemics—Addresses, essays, lectures.
 2. Discourse analysis—Addresses, essays, lectures.
 I. Bailey, Richard W. II. Title. III. Series.
 P160.P53   401'.41   81-9541
 ISBN 0-936534-02-08   AACR2

TABLE OF CONTENTS

Preface: Tagmemics and the Universe of Discourse viii
Introduction 3
I. Linguistic Complexity in a Two-Page Instruction Sheet 9
II. Levels of Observer Relationship in Verbal Art. 23
III. Grammar versus Reference in the Analysis of Discourse . . . 47
Bibliography 65

Tagmemics and the Universe of Discourse

Richard W. Bailey

A paradox captures a truth, and it is true if paradoxical that tagmemics is internationally among the best known of American linguistic theories and yet among the most neglected in the American academic establishment. The fame of tagmemics arises from the international work of the Summer Institute of Linguistics and its affiliated corporation, the Wycliffe Bible Translators. Within these two organizations, missionary-linguistics describe previously unwritten languages and translate the New Testament into them. According to his sister's estimate of almost a decade ago, Kenneth L. Pike and his colleagues had then schooled more than 10,000 students for the work of translation (E. Pike 1972:321); such students continue to travel to the remotest parts of the globe to carry on the practical work of description.[1] Although more languages have been studied from a tagmemic perspective than from any other, only occasionally have tagmemic descriptions been prepared for the well-known languages of Europe and Asia. Scholarly discussions of well-explored languages are little influenced by tagmemic principles; little-known ones are generally unaffected by other linguistic approaches.

In the first three decades of Pike's work—from 1935 to 1965—most

---

[1] Pike is quick to point out that not all members of the Summer Institute of Linguistics base their work on tagmemic principles, and there are many whose grammatical descriptions show the influence of other theories. Pike's emphasis on the need to study language in relation to society and behavior has, however, been particularly important in the work of SIL, and field workers have generally followed his ideas of studying language in its context rather than pursuing the idealizations emphasized by such other theories as generative-transformational grammar.

of his energy was devoted to encouraging the efforts of others and to the discovery of practical and easily comprehensible techniques that might enable persons with relatively little training to translate the Gospels. His books of this period on phonetics and intonation made him known to academic linguists in the United States and abroad, but his simultaneous efforts to encompass the continuity of language and behavior were much less generally influential. In recent years, he has encouraged tagmemic studies of English and occasionally compared tagmemics to such other theories as generative-transformational grammar, but the breadth of his views is still insufficiently appreciated by those who write introductory textbooks or publish technical papers in the major linguistic journals. In 1979, Thomas A. Sebeok was accurate in characterizing Pike's *Language* as a "heroic but neglected attempt at a unification of the structure of human behavior" (1979: 5).

Tagmemic theory arises from two intellectual streams, both of them distinctively American. The first emerges from the can-do spirit of Yankee ingenuity: problems of whatever kind can be rapidly solved with the application of that practical genius that Americans sometimes believe is a special national gift, a heritage of the frontier spirit. Although national confidence in American approaches to the solution of problems is somewhat diminished in the political and economic situation of our time, the conviction that problems can be solved, and the patterns of human behavior revealed, pervades tagmemic theory and the work of the missionary-linguists.

In his early work, Pike rejected the organization of linguistic study from smaller units to larger ones that was a hallmark of so-called post-Bloomfieldian linguistics: if the next level of linguistic structure could not be described until the level below had been perfectly analyzed—as the tenets of Bloomfieldian orthodoxy claimed—then how could the practical work of Bible translation go forward? Apart from practical objections to such a theory, Pike recognized that persons can learn a foreign language (and translate texts into it) only if they understand the cultural context in which language is used. Thus, tagmemics addresses language on all fronts at the same time. If there is no theory to account for a given "level," then some solution, however tentative, must be found to allow the work of description to go forward. Absolute perfection of the linguistic description, from the tagmemic perspective, is not of primary concern; the description is not to be judged solely against the standards of elegance, simplicity, and thoroughness but on the practical grounds of efficiency. Linguistic theory and linguistic description are proximate goals; the ultimate end is to bring the good news of the New Testament to those who have not yet heard it in their own language.[2]

When linguistic descriptions are viewed as means to an end rather than as ends in themselves, efficiency and rapid results gain greater importance. Pike himself, with two collaborators, translated the New Testament into Mixtec, the Middle American language to which he devoted his youthful field work. In promoting similar efforts in other languages, Pike's charismatic influence must be acknowledged. Through his famous "monolingual demonstrations," he shows how the rudiments of an unknown language can be quickly elicited and sketched. These demonstrations illustrate that efficient linguistic analysis can be accomplished quickly and without the help of written texts and a tradition of scholarly study. The demonstrations further display in the most dramatic way that a separation of linguistic levels is by no means the most natural entry point to understanding an unknown language. All of these tendencies reverse the priorities of more traditional academic pursuits: individual effort, prolonged study, and an emphasis on documentary evidence.

The second of the intellectual sources of tagmemic theory is similarly practical and arises from the empiricist tradition in Anglo-American scholarship. The community of tagmemic linguists is distinctive for a rejection of abstract entities unconnected to the material of language. *A priori* abstractions, in Pike's opinion, are necessarily removed from the data; their multiplication diverts attention from the source of answers to the linguist's questions. A culture transmits its language and its values through human contact, and the outsider must perceive language in its cultural setting. The data is there for all to see; tagmemics draws attention to ways of seeing.

For Pike and for tagmemics, language exists within a cultural matrix; it must not, he writes, "be treated in essence as structurally divorced from the structure of nonverbal human activity" (1967:26). In this orientation, Pike echoes the view of Saussure, who conceived of linguistics as part of semiology and of semiology as "a science that studied the life of signs within society" (1959:16). The social context of the language, the circumstances in which texts are produced, and the environment in which texts are evaluated and understood are thus primary to Pike's conception. None of these factors—production, text, and reception—can be ignored even provisionally for the analyst's convenience; all three are inextricable and to be understood

---

[2]Alan C. Wares, bibliographer for the Wycliff Bible Translators, reports that by 1980 SIL and Wycliff workers had produced translations of the entire New Testament into 128 languages; at least one of the Gospels had been translated into a further 225 languages (Wares, personal communication).

and described in their simultaneity.

From his earliest contributions, Pike has been fascinated by how language segments and sequentializes events that are neither discrete nor linear. While Pike and his colleagues are not noted for their attention to the visual arts, their preoccupation with multiple perspectives recalls the aesthetic experiments of the synthetic Cubists during the first decade of this century. Both tagmemists and Cubists have been puzzled and delighted by the transformation of multidimensional experience into two—or three—dimensional representation, and both insist that experience of the world is not authentically reflected in a single viewpoint. Through their works, the artists reminded viewers of the possibility of seeing experience in its unmediated wholeness; through his theory of language, Pike reminds all linguists that few elements in language serve a single function, that the seeming simplicity of language acts is not a fact but a function of our limited perspective and understanding.

As a corollary to his view that language cannot be divorced from the circumstances of its production and reception, Pike asserts that *signans* and *signatum* cannot usefully be separated. He rejects the tradition of study in which "form" and "content" (or "sign" and "meaning") are viewed as distinct entities. In tagmemics—and this is perhaps its hallmark—there are only form-meaning composites, and the dualisms of traditional studies have no place. *Tagmemes* themselves are form-meaning composites that are inherently indivisible and resistant to analysis by mechanical means.[3] Boundaries are often fuzzy rather than sharp, not only those that separate one linguistic unit from another but those that separate language itself from nonverbal behavior. Our perception of separation is also an artifact of our viewpoint, an inevitable human tendency to make sense of the world by organizing experience into units that we can grasp: these are consonants and those vowels, these hawks and those handsaws.

If the boundaries of linguistic units vary with each observer's perspective, it would appear that units can reflect no more than a consensus of viewpoints. Pike has been eager to avoid such extreme relativism, though he has been reluctant to separate units from their observation. In discussing this matter, he has found comfort in what

---

[3] The term *tagmeme* derives from Bloomfield's coinage to describe the "smallest meaningful units of grammatical form"; Pike, however, greatly modified Bloomfield's conception, first by dividing the aspects of the tagmeme into slot and class (thus subsuming Bloomfield's *taxeme*) but retaining Bloomfield's notion that the intersection of form and meaning constitutes a tagmeme. For a detailed chronology of the development of Pike's notion of the tagmeme, see Pike 1976.

physicists call "the granular nature of the universe," a conception that posits the existence of elementary particles as constituents of matter and energy. In tagmemics, this view is articulated as "the necessity of having dimensions to a point" (Pike and Pike 1976:31). A cluster of related variants in language can function as a "point" and stand in contrast to other clusters; the points themselves can be viewed as having "dimension" defined by slot, role, class, and cohesion. Tagmemes, like electrons, are theoretical primitives but gain their "reality" by matching observations of the real behavior of things in the world.

Since tagmemic theory is primarily concerned with ways of seeing, it must organize perceptions in a way that can be systematically applied in analysis. In exploring the problem of the observer's viewpoint, Pike has asserted that there are three discrete perspectives: particle, wave, and field (a metaphor drawn from the study of light). Any entity or group of entities can be perceived from each perspective—the first static, the second dynamic, and the third relational. While he claims that these three provide universals for the study of both verbal and nonverbal behavior, he has not attempted to justify them on the basis of the psychology of perception. For Pike, it is sufficient that they provide insight into analytic problems and contribute to solutions that allow for creativity and variation in human behavior. Once again, he finds himself articulating and elaborating an insight offered by Saussure: "Far from it being the object that antedates the viewpoint, it would seem that it is the viewpoint that creates the object" (1959:8).

While the orientation so far sketched has generally remained constant in Pike's linguistic theorizing, the development of tagmemic theory has undergone significant changes since he articulated it in the first part of his *Language* (published in 1954). Important ideas have evolved from that formulation and from the assumptions about phonology stated in his *Phonetics* (1943), *Phonemics* (1947), and *Tone Languages* (1948), particularly his recognition that linguistic boundaries are seldom as sharp as mechanical discovery procedures presuppose. The term *tagmeme* itself has varied somewhat in definition, though throughout it has remained an abbreviation for what Pike now commonly calls "unit-in-context." Hence, those working in tagmemics may draw on various stages of its development, elaborating an insight or writing a description from a point that Pike himself may have abandoned or elaborated in a different way. Since Pike asserts the dependence of observations on viewpoints, the growing diversity of tagmemics was a natural consequence of his fundamental assumption. Thus tagmemics has seldom enjoyed the benefits—or suffered from the liabilities—of an enforced orthodoxy typical of some other linguistic theories.

In the 1960s, Pike proposed to complement the perspectives of particle, wave, and field with a second dimension of three more terms: contrast, variation, and distribution.[4] The result is a matrix of nine cells—matrices are a recurring representational device in tagmemics—and the matrix is sometimes a theoretical assertion about facts as well as a heuristic device for organizing intuitions and observations.[5] Whereas post-Bloomfieldians proposed a sort of methodological *tabula rasa* for the linguist, on the assumption that prior intuitions are likely to distort the analyst's perception of linguistic structure, Pike recognized that even unfamiliar languages present familiar structures. In his view, the linguist cannot clear away all prior impressions, nor is there any reason for doing so. One function of the matrix is to organize first impressions and force observations into varying perspectives. The matrix thus functions as a heuristic device, one justified by efficiency in solving problems.

Since tagmemic theory shares with other analytic techniques a concern for repetitions in language and behavior, analysts are obliged to specify what counts as "the same" over time and space. In his early work, Pike explored in detail the contrast between *emic* units and their clusters of *etic* variants. Etic variants are grouped from some particular perspective, and thus they are explicitly defined by the nature and purpose of the inquiry. Such clusters are both an artifact of behavior—as when speakers of English recognize two pronunciations as the *same* even when they differ in virtually every phonetic detail—or an artifact of analysis—when, for instance, a sports writer compares the *same* team across a score of years even though all the personnel have changed. If groupings of etic variables were merely a conse-

---

[4]Though Pike remains interested in the intersections of particle, wave, and field with contrast, variation, and distribution, the resulting conception of the *tagmeme* with nine cells was relatively short-lived. However the development of this phase of the theory in the widely-read *Rhetoric* (Young, Becker, and Pike 1970) has influenced a variety of applications of tagmemics.

[5]Pike has been inclined to regard the typical matrix of a phonetic chart as a theoretical artifact; its rows and columns state the phonological structure of the language (or International Phonetic Alphabet). Other linguists (Bloomfield, for instance) have treated such displays as theoretically irrelevant. But the phonological matrix is not necessarily the only representation that Pike views as a mirror of structure. In many of his theoretical formulations, it remains unclear which displays are to be regarded as "facts of behavior" and which "artifacts of analysis." Consider, for instance, his claim of 1963: "The theoretical status of the matrix itself must now be treated in relation to its vectors; and we will conclude that *sometimes* a matrix must itself be treated as a well-defined emic unit" (my italics; Pike 1963:8).

quence of methodology or perspective, however, tagmemics would be entirely relativistic, its descriptions proliferating idiosyncratically. Pike rejects such relativism in principle, and he defines emic units (with their constituents) as actual properties of the verbal and nonverbal behavior under scrutiny.

In tagmemics, emic units are based on meanings as revealed in behavior. Rejecting the concept of meaning as a relatively abstract property of signs, Pike perceives meaning as actualized in the behavior of native speakers.[6] The analyst must make explicit the implicit meaning of the behavior of members of the community, recognizing that "a unit is *well-defined* when there have been specified its contrastive-identificational features, its variants, and its distribution in class, sequence, or other location and in a system of a universe of discourse" (Pike 1976:113). Hence, tagmemics aims primarily at distributional statements about language and behavior: repetition of "sames" (whether with sharp or fuzzy boundaries); clustering of variables within "sames" (whether predictable or free); operation of "sames" within some larger context.

Pike's vision of a complete description of any pattern of verbal and nonverbal behavior is clearly linked to the ideas of his mentor, Edward Sapir. For Sapir, language is primarily social, and access to its system is gained through study of its function in society. By emphasizing its role as communication between individuals, Sapir subordinates the function of language as expressive of emotions, thoughts, and desires. Language is a constant flow; thought is a variable with "its psychic value or intensity varying freely with attention or the selective interest of the mind" (Sapir 1949:14). Since in Sapir's belief, analysts have no direct access to mental processes, they are obliged to give special attention to social behavior which, when properly understood, yields insights into psychological processes. In this orientation, Sapir and Pike are fundamentally allied.

Pike's more specific debt to Sapir emerges from their common interest in the function of linguistic events. Sapir noted that the sound represented in English spelling as *wh* can function as the initial sound

---

[6]Since human behavior is creative, we cannot necessarily recognize the "meaning" of an event solely by comparing it with our previous experience (though such experience naturally plays a role in our understanding of it); hence, repetition is only one part of the definition of a meaningful unit. Since "behavior" may include verbal responses, nonverbal responses (e.g., applause), *and* mental responses invisible to the outsider, Pike is obliged to recognize mental states while maintaining his emphasis on tangible data. Hence, he occasionally resorts to such formulations as "semantics is not disembodied or abstract but always manifested, *at least by mental energy*" (my italics; Pike 1980, personal communication).

of such words as *which* and *why* but can also be produced by a person blowing out a candle (see Pike 1967:44). The physical sounds are the same; their functions are entirely distinct. Pike has elaborated this insight into the four-celled nexus of linguistic and behavioral units: slot, class, role, and cohesion. *Slot* and *role* are essentially defined from a functional perspective; both are syntagmatic in the classical sense, the first derived from analysis of the sequential arrangement of elements and the second from analysis of the "situation" in which the element occurs. At the opening of a telephone conversation, for example, an utterance may fill the slot of an "opening" and serve the roles of "greeting and self-identification." *Class* and *cohesion,* on the other hand, both consider the perspective of the physical manifestation of slot and role. The class of telephone greetings includes such alternatives as *Hello, Good Morning, ABC Corporation,* and *769-3738*; this class also includes silence and the recorded greetings of a telephone-answering machine. Class and cohesion both reflect the classical idea of associative relations; the former is concerned with utterances that seem "appropriate" to native observers (though some may be normal and some "off-norm"), and the latter points to implications and presuppositions. One greeting, in our example, will elicit friendly chatter; another the discussion of a commercial transaction.

Though Sapir, unlike Pike, did not organize his linguistic views into a set of postulates or definitions, close reading of Sapir's works reveals a conception that is elaborated in tagmemic theory. For instance, in Sapir's book *Language*, the same term, *form,* is used variously: for a sequence of meaningful sounds, for roots and affixes, for grammatical processes such as affixation or vocalic change, and for grammatical concepts (see Dinneen 1967:222). The fact that Sapir subsumed such usually distinct notions under the one term *form* reflects his idea that all of these aspects of language are variations of the same impulse, the human predisposition toward language use. In elucidating the *forms* of grammatical concepts, for example, he identified two classes: concrete concepts and relational concepts. The former includes radical and derivational concepts; the latter such concepts as reference, modality, personal relations, number, and time. All of these *forms* are subsumed in the tagmemic conception of a form-meaning composite.

In a tagmemic framework, any item (not excluding silence) is considered a form if it is included within "a hierarchical system of substitution classes" (Pike 1976:111). If, for instance, the articulation of *wh* is applied to extinguishing a candle, then its "substitution classes" include producing a gust of air by some other means or using a candle snuffer. If the articulation occurs in the English word *why*, then its substitution classes include *b* (in *buy*), *s* (in *sigh*), and a variety of others. Sapir was mainly interested in the place of this *form* in a linguistic system; Pike has generalized Sapir's idea to a broader descriptive field. Though there may be many hierarchies of substitution classes, Pike has proposed that there are three that incorporate all others: the referential (organizing the sort of information found in an encyclopedia), the grammatical (containing what Sapir recognized as concrete and relational concepts), and the phonological (incorporating the rules by which form-meaning composites are realized in the stream of speech). It is the essence of structure in each of its aspects that reflects, in Pike's view, the reality of language; the three hierarchies articulate the organizing impulse of all human behavior including language. As Sapir explained this essential point, "any concept that asks for expression must submit to the classificatory rules of the game" (1949:99).

Tagmemic descriptions have no necessary starting place (such as the sentence or the sound units of a language), but they do have a common goal: description of behavior within the context of a "universe of discourse." Of the many terms in use in Pike's theory, *universe of discourse* is perhaps the most vaguely defined. It incoprorates all of the "relevant" variables of a communication within a framework involving the participants (with their "relevant" traits of character and belief), their purposes (both over and covert), and the outcome of their exchange (whether or not it "succeeds"). All of the constituents of tagmemic theory—the nine-celled matrix of the heuristic, the four-dimensions of the tagmeme itself, the three hierarchies that organize referential, grammatical, and phonological form-meanings—are designed to make explicit the organization of human behavior in the universe of discourse.

Attempts to describe the universe of discourse are inevitably "heroic"; Pike's lifetime work challenges others who wish to explore the meaning of human behavior.

* *

The three essays that have been gathered in this volume provide an introduction to tagmemics directed especially to those who study signs within society. In his introductory overview, Pike explains the differing circumstances and audiences that gave rise to each essay and sketches some of the themes that unite them. As he notes, the second essay was prepared for presentation to the International Conference on the Semiotics of Art held in Ann Arbor in May 1978, a gathering made possible through a grant from the National Endowment for the Humanities. In editing these three papers for publication, I have been greatly assisted by Robin M. Fosheim. In preparing this "foreword," I have profited from the comments of Peter H. Fries, Kenneth L. Pike, and Edward L. Smith, Jr.; remaining flaws are my own.

References

Dinneen, Francis P., S.J. *An Introduction to General Linguistics.* New York: Holt, Rinehart and Winston, 1967.

Pike, Eunice V. "Pike—A Biographical Sketch." *Selected Writings.* Ed. Ruth M. Brand. The Hague: Mouton, 1972, pp. 321-24.

Pike, Kenneth L. "Theoretical Implications of Matrix Permutation in Fore (New Guinea)." *Anthropological Linguistics* 5.8 (1963), 1-23.

——— *Language in Relation to a Unified Theory of the Structure of Human Behavior.* 2nd ed. The Hague: Mouton, 1967.

——— "Toward the Development of Tagmemic Postulates." *Tagmemics: Theoretical Discussion.* Ed. Ruth M. Brand and Kenneth L. Pike. The Hague: Mouton, 1976, pp. 91-124.

——— and Evelyn G. Pike. "The Granular Nature of a Construction as Illustrated by 'Flying Planes'." *From Baudi to Indonesian.* Ed. Ignatius Suharno and Kenneth L. Pike. Danau Bira, Irian Jaya: Cenderawasih University and Summer Institute of Linguistics, 1976, pp. 29-37.

Sapir, Edward. *Language: An Introduction to the Study of Speech* [1921]. New York: Harcourt, Brace & World, 1949.

de Saussure, Ferdinand. *Course in General Linguistics.* Tr. Wade Baskin. New York: Philosophical Library, 1959.

Sebeok, Thomas A. *The Sign and Its Masters.* Austin: The University of Texas Press, 1979.

Smith, Edward L., Jr. "The Place of Tagmemics in Linguistic *Science.*" *The Fifth LACUS Forum* (1978), 540-54.

Young, Richard E., Alton L. Becker, and Kenneth L. Pike. *Rhetoric: Discovery and Change.* New York: Harcourt, Brace and World, 1970.

TAGMEMICS, DISCOURSE,
and
VERBAL ART

Introduction

In America we are living in a new linguistic era, and linguists have at last devoted themselves to the study of discourse. Discourse is tied to the society from which it has sprung, and linguists in this country have advanced toward treating language in the context of behavior. To linguists in Europe, or to linguists in America who were trained in Europe, the new focus of attention is not startling. Why the long delay? I suspect that it resulted from the craving of the Americans to make linguistics into a 'science,' even at the price of being isolated from psychology, divorced from the study of individual and social behavior, and estranged from the enjoyment of beauty. Perhaps the delay is also due to a fatal heritage from Plato, who predicated philosophy on a 'reality' composed of thought-features abstracted from source-particulars, from things-as-directly-known. Above all, the problem may have arisen from separating the things-in-themselves (or abstract features of things, situations, or events) from the reality of *person*—person as observer, person as reality, person as investing every 'thing-in-itself' with an *observer relation* as its discoverer, its watcher, or its deducer.

If somehow, we could take *particulars* as a component of reality in a deeper sense, without abandoning the simultaneous use of generalization, we would be like Heraclitus, who could both step and not step into the 'same' river; and we would be ready both to enjoy and analyze a particular poem and to search for linguistic structural bridges to link literature, for instance, with the study of grammatical rules for the utilization of prefixes, clauses, paragraphs, or style and genre markers. Literature could be joined with pleasure to linguistics to reveal patterns that would otherwise elude us.

I have been gradually heading in this general direction for three decades. But at the beginning my efforts were not a focused attempt to accomplish *this* task, but quite a different one—the analysis of unwritten languages in communities where no alphabet was available and no interpreter present to help the outsider. How could one find meaning there? Or words? *Only* in a context of behavior, gesture, and living—*and* in the telling of stories, folklore, or oral history. Our work showed that the 'standard' approach to linguistics through *written* language or with an interpreter involved us in a vast system of presuppositions not fully articulated by any linguist at the time. To teach beginners to face the challenge of these communities and their languages demanded our articulation of the assumptions and the methodology built on them; we had to devise a notation to preserve the results of the work and to make them available to those who were ready to work within our new frame of reference. Our work showed just how the observer's assumptions enter into a theory, not just into the perception of objects. And perception in turn affects the observer's view of the world.

More recently, I have asked myself how we can let literary scholars share the excitement of our discoveries about theories, communities and texts. These scholars are as busy as any linguistic bees and are wisely loath to waste time on ideas irrelevant to their pursuits. In this small volume, I hope to show them how the discoveries of our work can help them with theirs. Here I treat language not as *rules*, but as knowledge through words, jokes through words, joy through words, worship through words. Language bends us, moves us, drives us—or blocks us, holds us, binds us in a word-made mold. With language, by language, through language we act on our families, our friends, our nation—and revolutionize the world. Language is behavior—people in action, people dreaming, persuading, commanding. How can we linguists help others capture this tie that binds language to literature, to society, to philosophy?

The first of the three papers in this volume ("Linguistic Complexity in a Two-Page Instruction Sheet") was presented to the third annual convention of the Kentucky Interdisciplinary Conference on Linguistics, April 1, 1977, in a symposium on Language and Discourse Structure. But it grew out of work during the prior semester at the University of Michigan. That year I was director there of the English Language Institute, an organization designed to teach foreign students to better their control of English and to help them during their subsequent university studies.

Richard Young, chairman of the Humanities Department in the

College of Engineering (with whom Alton Becker and I had in 1972 co-authored a textbook on the teaching of English composition) had reported to us that some of our graduates from the Institute still had difficulty in understanding *technical written* English, even though their oral speaking ability was good. Why? In the fall of 1976 I ran a seminar to help teaching assistants in such programs to find out, and my contribution is embodied in this first chapter. (For some of theirs, see Pike, 1977b.) It should be easy to understand why I chose for analysis an item of 'engineering'—as complex as my mechanical ability allows: the assembling of a hamburger barbecue grill, purchased by my wife. I almost succeeded in putting it together; she only had to tighten the final screw after the first hamburger fell into the fire.

For that seminar and for this paper, I have tried to describe from a linguist's perspective some interesting phases of the instructions. In doing so, I was obliged to add to normal linguistics an analysis of the diagrams which formed an essential part of the instructions. The *arrangement* of the diagrams was a kind of nonverbal 'grammar,' something like the arrangement of words in a linear sequence in a story, but projected from the three-dimensional reality of the grill into two-dimensional space. How could the diagrams be matched with words, clauses, sentences, paragraphs—and warnings, urgings, omissions of the obvious, and the temporal sequence of joining the parts? What theory would have room for all of that, but retain a relationship to theory as already elaborated to address the myriad problems of learning foreign languages? Obviously, 'pure' linguistic science would have been hopeless, helpless—or simply blind to the demands of such a complex task. We had to integrate the author's *nonverbal* design with his verbal presentation for integration into the perspective of the foreign students.

Tagmemic theory is the only one known to me which has developed in such a way as to make such an integrated description immediately feasible. (I, however, assume that *any* theory can be pushed, bent and amplified by new axioms to meet new situations, wherever and whenever the will and dreams of its users demand them.) The theoretical basis for our theory is fully described in the references to publications by Pike (and collaborators) in the bibliography.

In this first article, our underlying assumptions begin to appear. The needs of the users and consumers of texts enter the theory through the referential hierarchy and, from a different perspective, through the grammatical hierarchy. At each stage of analysis, one sees *units* with their features of contrast (Aristotle should be happy), variation (hail to Heraclitus again), and appropriateness of distribution. In addition, there is the *perspective* of the *observer*—crucial to our philosophy of *emic* units, where the thing-in-itself is not known, but only items in relation to a human (or if you wish to add, as I do, also to a divine) observer. Each perspective incorporates a component which shows a static (particle) standpoint, a dynamic one (the wave view of the *same* thing, event or situation), and a relational view (the field).

Context, an essential frame for our descriptions, involves the tie of the concrete to relevance (meaning), or change of one unit to another, or of all units of a set to a universe of discourse. All of the units placed in their context can include hierarchical elements not only of grammar and reference, but also of phonology whether manifested as sounds, their alphabetical surrogates, or features that comprise diagrams.

The second paper is perhaps closer to the more usual interests of literary scholars. Entitled "Levels of Observer Relationship in Verbal Art," it was presented to the International Conference on the Semiotics of Art at Ann Arbor, May 6, 1978. Some of the same principles just described are once again relevant, as they *must* be if we are to claim that they constrain human perception, thought and imagination. If they can be omitted tacitly, as well as explicitly, they must be lowered in the theory from demands universal on the mind, to options.

The paper opens with emphasis upon the observer's importance to the definition of things or events; and, of course, several observers can be involved, hierarchically, in a particular event or in its being reported. The contribution of this paper is in a notation for these relationships—a notation grounded in the theory itself, and incorporating all of the concepts previously mentioned: unit, hierarchy, context and observer perspective. But why should any notation be important to someone interested in the literary language of a poem or story? Imagine an attempt to do multiplication or long division by using Roman numerals. I have tried, and failed, and unfortunately have not yet asked the mathematicians to teach me how to do it. In mathematics the extraordinary importance of notation type (including, of course, the concept of zero) can be clearly seen. What if something like that were available to literary scholars? I believe that a notation system for intonation provides just the information that is so hard to capture otherwise.

If a crucial part of what one means comes from one's intonation, *must the poet be forbidden to say what he means*? By recoding intonation contours, the poet could double his tools, with criss-crossing word-versus-pitch-meanings, more subtle than irony through words alone. Teachers could guide the ear of students on the pitch line.

The third article, "Grammar versus Reference in the Analysis of Discourse," is an expanded and revised version of a paper which I first prepared in 1978 in the Ivory Coast for joint publication by the University of Abidjan and the Summer Institute of Linguistics. Here I tackle a major theoretical problem: How can we demonstrate that in addition to phonology (or its orthographic representation) a text has two further structures, one of grammar and one of reference, both of which are concretely manifested? How can we show that the hierarchy of grammar is *distinct* from the hierarchy of reference? What kind of experimental evidence can support this view? Even within tagmemic theory, answers to these questions are not yet uniform, and the view presented here has been quite recently developed (see Pike and Pike 1972, 1977). This article argues that the telling structure of a story is often quite different from the happening structure of the events of that story, and demonstrates that fact by taking a simple story and retelling it in several different ways. The semantics is kept constant; the happening is not altered. But the fact of altering the linear (grammatical) order of telling forces many different grammatical devices to be used if the happening structure is not to be misrepresented or distorted.

Once more, notation enters: a brief sample of grammatical notation in tagmemic terms is shown to contrast with a sample of referential notation. Unfortunately, no complete analysis of the story can be given for either hierarchy—that would have made the article much too long. If, however, one wishes to see what the result might have been like one should examine the grammatical analysis of the story, "The Rich Young Man" (in Pike and Pike 1977: 12-20, 411-54), and a brief grammatical analysis with longer referential analysis of a story about a rabbit and a coyote, as told in the Mixtec language of Mexico (in the same work: 279-80, 367-77). For a more recent and more extensive treatment, the referential structure of a folktale at a Carib wake, with real actors entering the tale-while-it-is-told, and an extensive notational treatment, see Howland (1981).

Where do we go from here? Can such points of view in some way serve literary critics to help describe matters long studied by them? Some doctoral students have already begun to explore issues related to these views. Will composition classes expand their approach to include designed variability to increase student flexibility? Will more drama classes continue the work of Martin (with Pike 1974)? Can we somehow raise up a generation of intonation-controlling poets who will both write and read their own intonation? Answers to these questions will be provided in the next generation.

Kenneth L. Pike,
Dallas

Linguistic Complexity in a Two-Page Instruction Sheet

I. DATA SOURCE

An extraordinary amount of theoretical and metalinguistic apparatus is needed to describe a two-page set of directions for assembling a piece of household equipment. No simple set of rules of grammar will remotely cover it; nor can I do so in a short article. Units, hierarchies, context, and varying observer perspectives are all needed. I shall, however, indicate some directions such a detailed statement might take and suggest why a theory with at least the complexity of tagmemics is needed to approach directly many of the details involved.

Having purchased and assembled an outdoor barbeque grill,[1] I made a study of the problems which I had both in the actual assembly of the grill and in the attempt to analyze the linguistic structure of the instructions. [In order to facilitate reference to the document, I have added marginal section numbers to the instruction sheet (with my Section 7 being subdivided by the company's original numbers)]. I was interested in comparing this kind of discourse with the structuring of narrative (as described, for example, in Pike and Pike 1977). I wanted to find out what kind of differences in detail and in analytical problems exist between the two. Then, in a seminar at the University of Michigan, I assigned students to read the instructions, asking them to try to answer some of the questions I had raised, and to guess what difficulties foreigners might encounter in reading them.

---

[1]Assembly Instructions, Model 23C5, reproduced by permission of Barbecue Grills, Neosho, Missouri.

ASSEMBLY INSTRUCTIONS
Model 2305

2.1 IDENTIFY SCREWS AND NUTS HERE:

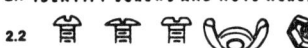

Round Head | Truss Head | Pan Head | Wing Nut | Lock Nut | Square Nut | Cap Nut | Grid Stud | Knob Cap | Spacer

3. SAVE THIS INSTRUCTION SHEET — Model and Part No. information required to order parts at a future date.

4. Tools required: Pliers, screwdriver, hammer

5. WARNING: HANDLE SHEET METAL PARTS WITH CARE TO AVOID INJURY.

6.
   6.1 Remove all parts from the carton. Do not discard the carton or packing until you have completed the assembly of your grill. When using the lock nut, be sure that it is threaded onto screw exactly as shown in Fig. A with open face of lock nut away from head of screw. If threaded on with open face toward head of screw, the lock nut will not hold tight.
   6.2
   6.3
      a   b

7. 1. Place BOWL (1) upside down on work surface. Attach BOWL CUP (2) to inside of bowl with three ¾" long panhead screws and lock nuts as shown in Fig. B.

   2. Attach ADJUSTMENT BRACKET (3) to bowl with one ¾" long panhead screw and lock nut as shown in Fig. B. (Use the hole near outer edge of bowl)

   3. Thread LIFTROD (4) thru adjustment bracket so that it appears as in Fig. B.

   4. Lower GRID TUBE (5) down thru hole in center of bowl until holes near end of tube line up with end of liftrod as in Fig. B. Slide inner end of adjustment bracket toward left until end of liftrod slides thru hole in end of grid tube. Attach inner end of adjustment bracket to bowl with ¾" long panhead screw and lock nut.

   5. Drive LIFT KNOB (6) onto outer end of lift rod with hammer. See Fig. B.

   6. The two LEG BRACKETS (7) are identical. Attach the short side of each leg bracket to the bowl with a ¾" long pan head screw and lock nut as shown. It is important that the leg brackets be positioned exactly as shown in Fig. B.

   7. Place a ¾" long pan head screw thru the hole in the bowl opposite the adjustment bracket. Thread the wing nut onto the screw but do not tighten until step 10. Wing nut should be on bottom side of bowl as shown in fig. B.

   8. Locate two TUBULAR LEGS (8) which have the section near the center of the leg crushed in as shown in Fig. C. These legs are identical. Place the two crushed portions of the legs together as shown so that the legs form an "X." When this is properly done, the two flattened ends of the legs will be as shown in Fib. C. Attach with a 1¼" long truss head screw and square nut through holes in center of leg. IT IS VERY IMPORTANT THAT THESE LEGS BE ASSEMBLED EXACTLY AS SHOWN IN FIG. C. Turn the legs over on a hard surface so that the head of the screw is downward and with a hammer flatten the end of the screw against the nut. This will assure that the nut will not loosen.

   9. Locate FRONT LEG (9). Insert 4¼" LONG ROD (10) through hole in the center of leg as shown in enlarged portion of Fib. D. Slide a TUBULAR SPACER (11) over each end of this rod so that you have a spacer on each side of the LEG (9) NOTE IN FIG. D. the relationship of the flattened end of LEG (9) to the flattened ends of LEGS (8). Now moving the two legs (8) open in scissors like action, guide the rod previously inserted through LEG (9) into position so that the ends of the rod will slip into holes in the two LEGS (8) as shown in Fig. D. Close the LEGS (8) over the ends of the rod.

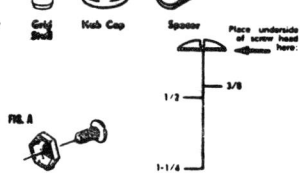

FIG. A

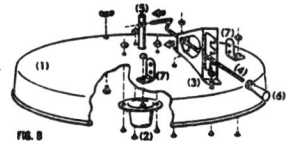

FIG. B

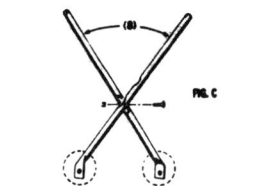

FIG. C

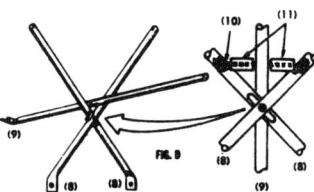

FIG. D

Linguistic Complexity in a Two-Page Instruction Sheet

10. Move the leg assembly on to the BOWL as shown in Fig. E. so that the LEGS (8) lay just inside of the LEG BRACKETS (7). Attach the legs to the leg brackets with ¾" long pan head screws and cap nuts. Tighten cap nuts as tight as possible. Guide slot in the flattened end of LEG (9) under the wing nut on bottom of bowl. Tighten wing nut to retain leg.

11. Slip large LEG CAPS (12) over end of EACH LEG as shown in Fig. F. Turn the unit upright.

12. Attach GRID STUD (13) to the GRID (14) as shown in Fib. G with a ½" long round head screw. Guide grid stud into top of grid tube. To raise grid, push downward on knob.

13. It is suggested that you remove grill grid from unit before folding. To fold unit, face the back of the unit, place foot at base of rear leg (8). Lift upward on bowl, and LEG (9) will come off of bowl. Allow unit to fold flat.

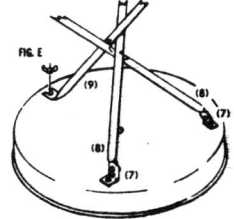
FIG. E

8. **ACCESSORIES:** See your local hardware or department store for safety glove, long handle tools, waterproof cover, etc.
9. **CAUTION:** If you use a liquid firestarter, follow closely the instructions given on the can. **DO NOT USE GASOLINE OR KEROSENE** as these are dangerous to use, can leave a bad taste in your food, and may damage the fine finish of your grill.
10. **DO NOT USE A CHARCOAL BURNING UNIT INDOORS DUE TO HAZARD OF CARBON MONOXIDE FUMES.**
11. **BURNING OUT YOUR NEW GRILL** —Your new grill should be burned out and allowed to cool before you cook on it. This allows the paint in the firebowl to set and rids the unit of fumes. Do not touch enameled surface during burn-out as paint will be soft until unit is cooled. Build normal fire for burn-out.
12. **USING A COAL BED** — A bed of pea gravel or charcoal base in your fire bowl will lengthen the life of your grill, save you charcoal and help create a draft under your coals for a smooth-burning fire. Such a coal bed should be replaced occasionally for maximum draft efficiency.
13. **RECYCLED NEWSPAPER** To conserve newsprint we are using old newspaper which we have bought from local civic groups for the purpose of wrapping parts.

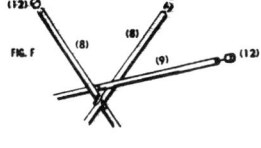
FIG. F

14. **TO ORDER REPAIR PARTS**
15. Tear off the bottom of this page at the dotted line. Write the number of parts desired in the QTY column next to the appropriate part number. When ordering painted parts indicate color preferred. We reserve the right to substitute colors due to availability. Fill out name, address and zip blanks. Enclose check or money order to cover cost of parts ordered. (Minimum order $1.00) Prices include postage. Allow 4 weeks for delivery. No C.O.D.

16. Send to: **BARBECUE GRILLS**
P. O. BOX 622
NEOSHO, MISSOURI 64850
Attention: Customer Service

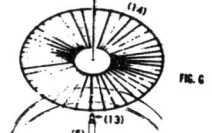
FIG. G

17.
PART - PRICE LIST MODEL 2305

KEY NO.	DESCRIPTION	PART NO.	COLOR	QTY	PRICE EACH	KEY NO.	DESCRIPTION	PART NO.	COLOR	QTY	PRICE EACH
1	BOWL	0024-2315			5.60	9	FRONT LEG	0023-2309			2.10
2	BOWL CUP	0030-2310			.40	10	4½" LONG ROD	0040-0546			.30
3	ADJUSTMENT BRACKET	0015-1832			.60	11	TUBULAR SPACER	0040-0661			.30
4	LIFTROD	0023-2314			.60	12	PLASTIC LEG CAP	0040-0155			.30
5	GRID TUBE	0023-2814			.50	13	GRID STUD	0040-0261			.30
6	LIFT KNOB	0040-0683			.40	14	SUNBURST GRID	P230-5010			5.30
7	LEG BRACKET	0023-1806			.30		SMALL HARDWARE PACK	2305-0030			1.20
8	TUBULAR LEG	0023-2308			2.00						
	BETTER HOMES & GARDENS BARBEQUE BOOK, 160 pages, 350 recipes, 136 illustrations							0040-0666			3.95

18. PLEASE FILL OUT COMPLETELY AND LEGIBLY.

19. SHIP TO: _____

   STREET _____

20. 0045-0174
   7510
   CITY _____ STATE _____ ZIP _____

II. REFERENTIAL PURPOSE OR EXPLANATION

In tagmemic theory of the Pike and Pike variety, the purpose[2] of an event belongs to its *referential* hierarchal structure, not to the grammatical construction which manifests it. The "why" of an event, or the "function" of a thing, is the *referential role* of that event unit or item unit. It is the set of such purposes and functions which drives speech, makes it relevant, and leads the speakers to talk. In this set of instructions there is one subset of purposes which—no matter how important—are almost entirely implicit, and there is a different subset which is explicit. Why the difference? The implicit purposes are those which, in general, the author of the instructions could assume the buyers would have before deciding to purchase the grill. Making them explicit would not help sell the item since the instructions are not seen prior to the purchase, (although they might be explicitly stated in advertisements). For example, one does not need to be told in the assembly instructions: *This grill is made for you to cook steaks on,* since one knows this before purchasing the grill and reading the instructions. Similarly, one need not be told, *Take this step in order to assemble the grill*; the purchaser knows before buying the grill that he is to assemble it and must follow the steps prescribed if he is to succeed. All of this is implicit in the title, (1.1) *Assembly Instructions.*

Explicit purposes are stated throughout the instructions. One set of them anticipates the possibility that the reader might fail to follow the directions through ignorance, carelessness, oversight, or by assuming that some detail is more or less irrelevant. Warnings are often given with the stated purposes: for example, (5) *Warning: handle sheet metal parts with care* [in order] *to avoid injury.* Another set does not concern the assembly directly, but anticipates the initiation of the grill: (11) burning out the grill to set the paint; (12) lengthening grill life by appropriate draft. As an aside irrelevant to the grill itself, there is (13) an explanation concerning the seller's use of old newspapers for packing (a conservation measure). For the more distant future, there is (14) a series of instructions for ordering spare parts and (3) for saving the assembly instructions sheet for this purpose.

Throughout the instructions there are a few hints of explanation as to the relation between particular steps: implicit at the end of (6), a step to be taken to avoid the loosening of a screw; (7.1) a suggestion that one see the figure; (7.8 end) an action to be taken so that a nut

---

[2]Perhaps the single most important development in our recent tagmemic theory is the addition of purpose as a criterion in the referential hierarchial structure of a reported event. One purpose can be subordinate to a higher level purpose, which in turn is subordinate to a further one. This contribution is from Evelyn G. Pike.

will not loosen; (7.9) a sequential reason—to place the spacer properly so that the rod will fit; (7.10) direction to tighten the nut in order to retain the leg. Note also the implied hierarchy of purpose in (7.13): *first* one faces the back of the unit, and *then* one lifts upward on the bowl, in order to fold the unit.

In addition to the referential function of events, the referential function of items is occasionally made explicit, as in (7.5), *drive . . . with hammer*. In this text, an item with its functional role is lower in the referential hierarchy than an event with its purpose. Deborah Tyma, a student in the seminar, pointed out that the author chose to specify purposes for some items and not for others; this choice, she added, indicates the writer's opinion of his probable audience. In my own words: the author did not assume that the assemblers need instruction in the appropriate use of common tools ([4] pliers, screwdriver, hammer).

III. NONLINEAR REFERENTIAL PRESENTATION OF CHRONOLOGICAL SEQUENCE VERSUS GRAMMATICAL PRESENTATION

In tagmemics we make a crucial theoretical difference between the grammatical hierarchy and the referential one. In a normal instance of reporting a single event in time, the two are potentially isomorphic with coterminous borders. But when simultaneous events are being reported, isomorphism is impossible since descriptions must be sequenced in the report. In some cases, a chronological or logical sequence can in English be partially or completely changed in presentational order (e.g. told backwards); when this is done, the referential structure of the tale is unaffected, but the grammatical structure of the telling is radically altered. Grammatical order is necessarily *linear* (since words come out of the mouth one at a time), but referential order is at least potentially simultaneous.

Describing a static situation presents problems parallel to those of presenting an event involving change or movement. Both static and dynamic events are made linear in grammatical presentation even if the items or events are, referentially speaking, simultaneous in space or time.

Many of the directions in this set of instructions (e.g., 7) imply the need for future events in a stated order. But in the instructions as a whole, there are radical departures from chronology. Why? First, in (3), the reader is warned, *before* he has used the sheet, not to throw it away (i.e., *later*). The author presumably anticipated the assembler's failure to read remarks which follow the assembly instructions. If this warning occurred in the "normal" sequential place (at the bottom of the last page), the assembler might neglect to read it. In (5) a general warning is given which applies to the entire process—that is, to handle metal parts with care. In (6), the reader is told not to discard the box or packing paper until finishing the assembly (since some part might still be hidden in the paper). In (2) a list of screws and nuts, with their names, is given before they are required for use. The author presumably presented this list before giving the assembly instructions to aid the assembler in the selection process later. Similarly, in (4) a list of tools is given before each is required and before their functional role is explicitly stated (as in 7.5, *with hammer*, as indicated above).

IV. PRINCIPLES OF TAGMEMIC THEORY ILLUSTRATED BY THE INSTRUCTIONS

Before further discussing the difficulties of chronology and assembly, I will illustrate briefly some of the crucial components in tagmemic theory:

A. **Unit.** Units of various sizes and relevance are described in the instructions. At the top of the part-whole hierarchy is (1.2), the grill itself—unnamed except by model number. On a lower level, the names and diagrams for screws, nuts, and other equipment are given (2).

1. *Contrast.* The author differentiates types of screws—in (2.2) by diagram and in (2.3) by name. Round head, truss head, and pan head are distinguished from one another; and, as a subset, wing nut, lock nut, square nut, and cap nut are differentiated. Note that the shapes of the heads and the shapes of the nuts are contrastive features within the set.

2. *Variation.* There is a degree of flexibility specifically indicated in the instructions. Attached to the initial instructions was a small slip saying: *NOTICE: Use 1/4" long panhead screws in place of 3/8" long panhead screws on instructions #1, 2, 4, and 6. This unit is packed with seven 1/4" panhead screws.* That is, the class of screws itself is variable in terms of usable parts. Similarly, on the level of the grill as a whole, there is variability in terms of form: it can be folded for carrying, or the lift rod can be set in different places to determine the height for different cooking purposes (7.3).

3. *Distribution.* There is *appropriateness* of parts in relation to the whole—that is, distribution of the elements in a system. The screws are indicated as having particular locations; these are often indicated not in words, but in diagram (as in Fig. B).

B. **Hierarchy of parts in relation to whole.** The grill itself comprises a total unit, with parts either to be joined in sequence or in subassemblies later added to the whole: for example, the rod (Fig. B—Item 4) must be added to the adjustment bracket (Item 3) before the combination is added to the bowl (otherwise the rod would be impossible to attach to the grid tube [Item 5]).

1. *Referential hierarchy.* We noted earlier that the author chose to describe the purposes of some items while ignoring others. Many more descriptions could be added. For example, legs are given so that the bowl can stand above the ground for the cook's convenience, but this is not explicitly stated. The chronologically numbered sequence of instructions—in the sheet itself (7)—is also part of the referential hierarchy.

2. *Grammatical sequence.* Analysis of the presentation of the material reveals classes of words (nouns, verbs, and so on), noun phrases, clauses, sentences, paragraphs, and sections. Within (7), the sequential numbering emphasizes the linearity of this grammatical presentation.

3. *Graphic hierarchy (a surrogate for phonology).* In speech we analyze sounds, syllables, stress groups, and higher units. In written material, however, we deal with letters or printed materials on the page. Note that in the instructions there is a hierarchy in letter size and type style. Both the lower case and upper case are relatively small in (7). On the other hand, there are larger, heavier caps in (3) and (5), and still larger caps in the title. The caps in (2.1) have special spacing. In (8) through (10) they are relatively small but in bold face. Still smaller caps are found in (18). In addition, these letters enter into written words, which in turn enter into written sentences, and then into sections, and sections of sections. As a total set, these types comprise an n-dimensional taxonomy which could be illustrated by a matrix.

C. **Context.** Nothing is significant by itself. An object or event acquires meaning only after it is viewed within a larger structure.

1. *Form-meaning composite.* The words on the instruction sheets are not randomly mixed on the pages. They are put into combinations which are intended to signal some meaning to the hearer. Language shows up as a form-meaning composite both in specific grammatical forms—for instance, meaningful phrases and clauses—and in the referential structures of purposive events and relevant items and situations.

2. *Change through a shared component.* Items affect one another only when they share a context—by bumping or merging or by being part of a pattern. In (7.5), the hammer's contact with the other items effects a change: *Drive LIFT KNOB (6) onto outer end of lift rod with hammer.* The warning to beware of injury from

sharp metal in (5) is actually a warning to avoid contact with its edges.

3. *Universe of Discourse.* One's interpretation of written and spoken material is influenced by one's total expectancy; it is only in reference to some kind of genre, style, or situation, personal background experience, or thought pattern that the material can "make sense." We have already mentioned that the purchaser had expectations in advance. The assembly instructions (1.1) therefore "make sense" specifically in relation to this larger universe of discourse of the purchaser.

D. **Multiple Perspective.** Items can be looked at from various view points. Thus, a comprehensive analysis of the assembly instructions requires that we take account of the observer—both the writer observing the audience in his imagination, and the audience observing the instructions, the parts, and the packing materials. Each must have a clear idea of the other if successful communication is to be effected.

1. *The static view (particle):* Here one looks at parts in isolation from one another—or else at the names or diagrams for those parts. In (2.2), for instance, the reader views a list of the kinds of screws and nuts apart from the other items. On a higher level in the referential hierarchy, events which are purposive are also units and can be abstracted from a total sequence and looked at by themselves. Although in reality events are often inseparable, the observer assumes otherwise when considering them from the static perspective.

2. *The dynamic view (wave).* Here the observer looks at the assembly process as a series of events. Attention is directed to the changes which occur within the process, the ways in which the events overlap or merge, and the ways in which they influence one another. Any single event may be viewed as having a beginning, a middle, and an end (like a wave). Sometimes one part of an event (the nucleus) is more prominent than other parts (marginal elements). In the referential hierarchy a small sequence, such as the tightening of a nut, may be an early part of a larger sequence, wherein one part of the equipment is attached to the bowl, which eventually serves as a pan to hold charcoal, which in turn will be burned in order to cook food—the end purpose of assembling the grill.

3. *The relational view (field).* From this point of view the observer is interested in the relationships between items. We now begin to get the payoff in graphic terms from Figures B, C, D, E, F, and G of the instruction sheet. Instead of trying to put into a grammatical linear sequence of words the specific way in which these items are

related, the author provides diagrams which label various parts to show their relationships. This field view of some of the parts is far more clear than a simple statement in words would have been. The representation of an extremely intricate space-relational situation by a grammatical linear sequence of words can sometimes be more confusing than helpful.

When one takes the field viewpoint, the static and dynamic elements must also occasionally be considered at the same time for a clear understanding. In Figure D, for example, the legs are shown as separate items; but from right to left in the figure there is an arrow showing *change* (wave) possibilities. A similar technique is employed in Figure C. And in Figure B (4.5) a heavy arrow at the top shows the lift rod being moved into the grid tube. In addition, dots in Figure B connect items which would otherwise be invisible (the screws would be under the bowl, for example), and items which are obscurely related to each other (the wing nut above the bowl at the top of the Figure, for instance, is shown with dots to be related to the screw below the bowl).

V. PROBLEMS IN THE ASSEMBLY

In the previous section I showed how the instructions were related to components of the tagmemic theory: unit, hierarchy, context, and perspective. I will now discuss the same list of theoretical elements and show how failure to understand any one of them might give trouble to readers (here represented by my own reactions and those of my students).

A. **Unit.** I had difficulty with contrast. I could not differentiate some of the screw types since the list of materials in the instructions differed from the materials actually supplied—and the appended note revising the list did not account for all the changes or substitutions in the actual materials. I could not match some of the parts to the diagrams. In addition, a bolt for me has never been a variety of screw—and the reference to bolt as screw in (2.1-2) left me uneasy for just a moment.

▼ariation was present, and yielded difficulty, in that the instructions as a whole had been modified by the additional note.

As for distribution, the outline form of the material did not trouble me. The sequence seemed very appropriate to the data and to my needs as they arose.

B. **Hierarchy.** More problems arose with the referential hierarchy. Purpose enters here, and sometimes I felt uncomfortable (but not handicapped) in assembling the grill since I did not obtain from the instructions the *reason* for a few contrastive differences. I was not told, for example, why a lock nut was used in some places, a square nut in others, and a cap nut in still others. What would I have done if some of these had been the ones omitted?

As for the grammatical hierarchy, a highly competent foreign student—Dirk Panhuis from the Netherlands—was forced to read the material slowly since it was difficult for him. This caused him on occasion to interpret one part of speech for another or one role of a word for a different one. At first, for example, he thought *Lower GRID TUBE* (5) referred to a grid which was lower—presumably an error he would not have made if the grammar of the instructions had not been in a special abbreviated style (i.e. if it had said *Lower the grid tube*).

The relation between grammatical and referential hierarchies is often a source of difficulty in many kinds of texts. Grammatical structure is linear; one item stated after another in sequence. But the data to be presented is *n*-dimensional, in network relations, with spatial directions up or down, right or left, and front or back, and time relation sometimes sequential and sometimes simultaneous. Since grammar can do none of this efficiently, reading is often difficult. With the instructions, the diagrams are extremely helpful; imagine, for example, putting Figure B into words. An extensive paraphrase, such as the following, would be necessary to cover even a small part of it:

> Take a lift rod (identified as a rod of iron about a quarter of an inch thick, two feet long, with one end bent to a 45 degree angle, following which an inch later it is bent in the opposite direction to a 45 degree angle, so that there is a three-inch long hook at the end of the rod); take the adjustment bracket (which is an attachment about eight inches long, made of diagonally-shaped sheet metal, with the ends bent at right angles to the plate, and then with these bent bits—an inch wide—containing a further flap about an inch long bent up at right angles; in each of these little flaps there is a hole for a screw to enter to attach to the inverted bolt . . .

This is incomplete and inadequate. Why? In my view, because words must come in *linear* grammatical order; but much of our perception is n-*dimensional*. Hence diagrams are sometimes more useful than words, if accompanied by words interpreting them appropriately. This inherent difficulty was handled well in the instructions: the diagrams interpreted by words, and words illustrated by diagrams, helped link grammar and reference together. Nevertheless, Gregory McCoy wished that a diagram of the finished product had been included in the instructions to show the total number of units as parts of a larger system. This, he felt, would help in the movement toward the final goal of the assembly.

The phonological hierarchy gave fewer problems. This was so because most of the phonology was in a helpful orthographic surrogate—different sizes of letters, paragraphing, numbering, diagrammatic style. But Panhuis, the foreign student, had a slightly different problem. With no clues in our orthography for certain stress placements and groupings of stress, he occasionally missed a meaning completely. For example, in 7.9 he could not understand: *Now moving the two legs open in a scissors like action.* How can *scissors* be *like* action? But then a friend pronounced the whole with the right rhythm—not as "scissors, like action" but as "scissors-like action;" he would have been helped if it had been worded as "open like scissors in action," where the grammatical order would not have allowed the misreading in the phonology.

C. **Context.** We have already partially covered the problems of relating form to meaning in a composite. That is what the instructions are all about—and when difficulties have arisen it has been because of difficulties in recognizing the intentions of the author in the forms he used to convey them. For instance, difficulties arise when there is variation of meaning with constancy of form. Ann Wehmeyer was slowed down by the author's specialized technical meanings for everyday words. She was unaccustomed to thinking of "threaded" (in *threaded onto a screw* 6.3) as a mechanical term—presumably associating the term with sewing. And she was uncomfortable with the use of "guide" in *guide grid stud into top of grid tube* (7.12), being more familiar, perhaps, with "guiding a person *to* a place."

While reading the assembly instructions, the students and I experienced a number of changes. For instance, our knowledge about the grill increased, but sometimes, the author's lack of clarity caused us to become frustrated. Thus, the author affected us through the diagrams and text, and the process illustrates the notion of change through shared components.

We noted earlier that the reader's universe of discourse had to include some idea of the author's expectations. I had to believe, for example, that the instruction were not a fictional statement and that it was really possible for all the things to work out right.

D. **Perspective.** It was not always easy for us to get the appropriate spatial perspective on the individual particles in the diagrams. Beverly Fried thought that Figure B was too cluttered and the characters too small, making it difficult for her to distinguish holes from screws or arrows.

The wave perspective entered in reading. As Dycus pointed out, one had to struggle to figure out just where one was in the stages of completeness. For this, I found the arrows to be helpful in pointing out a *before*, an *after*, and a *change*—a wave component. But Edward Smith found Figure D misleading, since it was drawn with the legs already "scissored," though the text referred to them as being parallel (7.9). A clear wave sequence is crucial to one's understanding in such situations.

The field perspective helps us to verbalize other problems inherent in the task of assembling the grill. There was an "exploded" diagram, as part of Fig. B, to help the reader "see" some things which were in fact invisible. Unfortunately, the author did not explain this and I lost considerable time in figuring it out. Similarly, the arrow in that figure was not explained in the text and this too caused difficulty. In spite of these problems, Figure B is an elegant, compact fusion which gives simultaneously a particle view of elements, a "blueprint" field structure of the whole, and a dynamic implication of movable parts as wave. It was the degree of condensation, not the conception as such, that gave me trouble.

A different instance of condensation bothered Janice Bogan. Speaking of 7.1, she said, "We are told to place the bowl upside down on a table, then to attach something to the inside of it. Are we to do this through the table?" And the instruction to put a wing nut on the bottom side of the bowl (7.7) also confused her. "What side was considered by the author to be the bottom?" she wondered. "Is it the side which will be the top when we're all finished, or is it the bottom of what now is the top?"

Somehow, the reader must be able to know what angle he is looking from and what angle the author is talking from. If these shift during the author's discussion, the reader may have difficulty in relating the two, as Dycus did in 7.9: "The diagram [Figure D] was extremely hard to understand and did not help much. The enlarged portion is sitting at a different angle than the basic diagram so I lost the relationship between the tubular legs (8) and the front leg (9) with its long rod (10)—all to be attached upon completion of step 7.9."

VI. IMPLICATIONS

What might a literary scholar gain by watching me and my students solve this simple problem? A simple set of concepts—neither new nor startling in themselves—have been applied *as a system* to the description of a nonliterary product—a commercial presentation of instructions. This system came from a radically different kind of experience: the attempt to teach thousands of persons to study unwritten languages, to reduce them to writing, to make dictionaries, and to analyze their vastly different grammatical patterns. Components of this theoretical view have been used—in part—by members of the Summer Institute of Linguistics who are currently studying some seven hundred different languages in all the continents of the world. At the same time, this theory can be used to describe and illuminate problems of native speakers trying to follow every-day directions. Surely a theory with such widespread applicability must capture something of the psychology of human beings. And this should tease literary scholars. It should make them wonder if some developing aspect of the system could be helpful in resolving some of the problems they face in the analysis of the more elegant articulations found in literature.

Levels of Observer Relationship in Verbal Art

This is one of the most exciting decades in history for linguistics: the broad range of theories and many sources of input available to us encourage flexibility and new directions in our approach to language. But our perspective must be vastly wider than linguistics. It must be multicultural within the academic scene. The Conference on the Semiotics of Art in Ann Arbor, May, 1978 (to which this paper was presented), amply demonstrated that fact. The massive bibliographical references given by Thomas A. Sebeok not only there, but in many publications elsewhere, summarize for the linguist the vast riches in semiotic literature over the centuries. In this paper I will mention a few of the talks given at that Conference which seem to impinge most directly on the subject of this paper: levels of observer relationship in verbal art, with special attention to varieties of author-reader (or speaker-listener) interaction.

I. THE OBSERVER IN RELATION TO THE VERBAL OBJECT.

Verbal art should be viewed as a two-phase event involving at least two participants: the one who prepares or delivers the art, and the one or many who receive it. Without this two-way process—action and reaction—the total artistic event has not "occurred." Ciardi claims that "the badness of bad poetry can always and only be located in the quality of the sympathetic contract" (1959:847). Clearly, his point is that the "receiver" of poetry is responsible to a great extent for the artistic quality of the poem. In his view the reader must share the poet's underlying belief or value system—even if only temporarily and in the imagination. If a reader is unable to sympathize with the author, the poem will be a bad one for that reader.

Ciardi's point may be generalized to include *all* objects of human experience. An object or event is described by human beings in relation to some standpoint which they adopt—consciously or subconsciously—as a point of reference for their description. Without a belief system, without an underlying emotional relation to the universe, without some standard of beauty or acceptance, some assumption (tacit or explicit) about the nature of the universe, no experience can be sanely human. Thus, one's experience of any object is always accompanied by an attitude, and to some extent the experienced object takes on the color of that attitude.

This view leads to a further assertion: each observer of an art event is a participant in that event, and by virtue of their mutual participation in an event, author and observer are related. This basic relationship I call a social one in relation to verbal art. Observers differ in their reactions because they have different biographies, potential differences (major or minor) in their belief systems, underlying emotional systems, and value systems. Each of these contributes to what I call "dynamic vectors of experience" (see Pike and Pike 1977:365-75). Each person sees an event from his own viewpoint. Therefore, in describing an observer's behavior, that observer's viewpoint must become part of the description, and a separate description must be given for the dynamic experience of each observer. The notion of different dynamic vectors of experience will enter into our discussion of the different levels of relationship between the author or performer of art and the receiver of that art.

I was myself very late in coming to understand that evaluative and interpretative statements about art are neither right nor wrong; they simply are. I recall when I first met a particular graduate student (one who was highly competent and a recipient of prizes for creative writing), I casually mentioned something about Blake's poem concerning a worm in a sick rose (in Erdman 1968:23). I took it for granted—as he saw—that roses were good but that worms-in-roses were bad because they destroyed the roses. The student protested that he "liked the worm!" Similarly, in a committee discussing a thesis about a certain poem, I asked, "Why not ask the poet himself?" To my well-intentioned question, the chairman replied, "He wouldn't know!" And most recently, in preparing for this paper I was perusing for the first time a book by Richards on poetry and was startled to see that Richards had collected radically different evaluations of poem after poem (1929:19-170). Although I continued to feel a certain outrage at a universe which could allow such divergent and conflicting opinions as to what good art must be, I clearly could not control that universe. My inevitable alternative was to accept divergent interpretations and evaluations of artistic material. This had at least one compensating emotional characteristic: it allowed me to dislike intensely some poems without having to "prove" they were bad or give *rational* reasons for my aversion. I could simply claim that I was not in a "sympathetic contract" with that author.

II. PRELIMINARY DIFFERENTIATION OF GRAMMATICAL AND REFERENTIAL STRUCTURES

My new perspective on poetry led me to apply to poems a recent development in linguistic theory which I used with my co-author Evelyn Pike (1977) in analyzing the structure of folk tales, non-narrative, descriptive, and scientific material. A brief explanation concerning the approach and notation of this theory is needed before discussing its applicability to poetry. Specifically, I will describe a *unit-in-context* in terms of four characteristics: 1) its specific placement in a larger (syntagmatic, sequential) structure; 2) the class or set of classes (words, clauses, utterances, etc.) to which it belongs as a member of the larger structure; 3) its function or role in relation to the other parts of the structure; and 4) its cohesion with other parts of the structure.

Box 1 WHERE (nuclear or marginal in the sequence) [= Slot]	Box 2 WHAT or WHO [= Class]
Box 3 WHY [= Role or Function]	Box 4 HOW RELATED (in code, frame of reference, universe of discourse, in time, space, or anaphora) [= Cohesion]

Figure 1. Four characteristics of a unit-in-context (Tagmeme).

Let us take these four characteristics and put them into a framework. In Figure 1, we label the cells as Box 1, Box 2, Box 3, and Box 4. Each box refers to one of the four characteristics, and together they describe one unit-in-context. Box 1 refers to the specific placement of the contextual unit in a larger structure. In identifying the placement of a contextual unit, we specify whether it occurs at a point of prominence in the larger syntagmatic structure (the nuclear point), or at a less prominent point (a marginal point). We look at the whole structure as a *dynamic wave* (with a beginning, a middle, and an end), and we specify *where* the unit-in-context occurs on the wave. In technical terms, we say we are identifying the *slot* that the contextual unit fills.

Box 2 specifies *what* or *who* is in the slot. Usually a contextual unit is a member of some class or set of classes, so in technical terms we say that Box 2 specifies the *class* of the item which fills the slot. A class of items is characteristically permitted to occur in specified places of the larger sequential structure, but not in other places. Thus, knowing the class helps us to characterize the structure as a whole. If we look at a class of items in isolation (apart from position in an including sequence), Box 2 gives a static view of the materials.

Box 3 tells us the *function* or *role* of the contextual unit in relation to other parts of the sequential structure. When describing a unit in the referential hierarchy, Box 3 can be thought of most easily as indicating *why* that unit is used.

Box 4 refers to a number of features, all of which emphasize a relational view of language and fall under the heading *cohesion*. This box tells us *how* the contextual unit relates to its own constituents and to the other parts in the larger sequential structure. It specifies the way in which the unit controls (or governs) the other parts, and the way in which it is controlled by others. Finally, this box is used to indicate the appropriateness of the contextual unit as it occurs in the structure.

In technical terms, the total unit-in-context with these four characteristics is called a *tagmeme*.

Although the same display can be used for grammar and reference, there is a sharp difference between them. The grammatical display shows *linear* structure, the order in which the tale is told. The referential structure of a tale indicates the *happening* order rather than the telling order. When one says *John came home, then he ate his supper,* the order of telling and the order of happening are the same. But one can also say *John ate his supper after he came home,* in which case the happening order (or the referential structure) is unchanged, but the telling order (or the grammatical structure) is reversed.

Reference and grammar become even more distinct when simultaneous events are reported. Many things can happen at the same time, but they can only be stated one at a time since they must be "mapped upon" a linear telling order of grammar. Of course a linear grammatical presentation allows for alternatives in the telling order: one complete happening may be told before another, or bits and pieces of the events can be taken and interwoven in some fashion. If the listener is not to be confused, there must be some way of indicating where the pieces were taken from so that their total referential structure can be reconstructed in the mind of the listener.

Another major difference between reference and grammar is found in the semantic components of each. The semantic component of grammar involves *general* relations. For instance, in the clause "Bill shot the tiger," the actor (Bill) is related to the undergoer (the tiger) through an action (shot), and both actor and undergoer are related to the action. In the referential hierarchy we are more interested in the "encyclopedic" or specific character of the event. We're not only interested in the fact that Bill is an actor, but in the fact that it is a *particular* Bill who is the son of a particular man, living in a particular time and era. The semantics of the referential hierarchy capture the particularity and paraphrasability of the item or event.

In the referential hierarchy—unlike the grammatical hierarchy—we find a place for handling truth and error. The equation $9 + 4 = 1$ is grammatically acceptable in that it has the proper structure needed for an equational sentence. But referentially it is false in ordinary arithmetic. However, if we're talking about an hour hand sweeping around the face of a clock showing twelve hours, then 9 hours plus 4 more hours gets the hour hand back to 1 o'clock, and it is true that nine plus four equals one. Thus we must specify whether we are thinking of a clock or of an arithmetical line. Truth or falsehood may be specified in relation to such a background system and identified in Box 4.

We can now see that two observers with opposing points of view can both be correct, relative to their respective frames of reference. Tagmemics accounts for different points of view in its formulas, and it is this feature of the theory which makes it especially applicable to verbal art. The "sympathetic contract" which Ciardi posits between author and audience can (and must) be specified in tagmemic formulas. We must specify the points of reference for both participants *before* we can know whether the reader will consider a particular poem to be good or bad. The sympathetic contract must be written into the formula or we cannot evaluate poetic pleasure or displeasure.

III. VIEWPOINTS ABOUT THIS PAPER

The preceding assumptions can affect our view of this particular paper itself. An event occurred in which Richard Bailey asked Pike to prepare and present this paper. This can be seen from Pike's view (i.e., as Pike's vector) as the dynamics of his experience.

The fact that Bailey asked Pike to do this is indicated in Box 2 of Figure 2, Section A, Unit-in-Context (1). In Box 3 the reason for Bailey's request is guessed at (to broaden topics at the conference). In Box 1 reference is made to Bailey's biography into which this event fits (with no guess given as to its specific placement in his biography). A more solid guess (hence with no question mark) suggests in Box 4 that this decision was reached in relation to Bailey's double interest in linguistics and literature.

In the second unit-in-context of the same section, Pike's acceptance and preparation are specified as marginal to the main event. Belief systems about language and behavior affect any presentation or discussion. My own postulates (see Pike, in Brend and Pike 1976:91-127) include emphasis on the possibility of *any* unit being seen from one of several points of view—e.g., as static, dynamic, and relational (or as particle, wave, and field). This is indicated in Box 4 of A.2 because it affects (or governs) unit-in-context 3—my discussion of the sympathetic contract between speaker and listener.

The oral presentation itself is nuclear to the event, and is indicated as being so in Unit-in-Context 3 of the same section. Post-marginal components (e.g., the submitting of the written form) are not mentioned, but a place is left for them in the sequence with a Unit-in-Context 4 indicated by dots.

Section B of Figure 2 (Bailey's view of the event) overlaps considerably with Section A, both because the action is in part the same, and because I am having to make the guesses in both instances. However, there is a substantial difference in the marginal situations leading up to the talk since they differ for Bailey and Pike. In Section C of Figure 2, I have suggested that one of the audience, a Mr. X, might have had motivations differing from others of the audience (see Box 3 of C.2). Backgrounds and convictions (Box 4) differ, and such differences allow useful discussion to develop in a meeting. It is precisely the fact that one cannot always anticipate what the result of these differences or background will be which sometimes makes such a discussion interesting.

Figure 2 illustrates features of the event that I consider to be important, since I was the one who constructed the tagmemes. But it also succeeds in accounting for points which others stress in their theories of artistic events. At the Semiotics Conference, Benjamin Hrushovski insisted repeatedly that author and reader have potentially different frames of reference for their perceptions, and that the characters in a work presented or read by them have still different frames of reference (1978). This fact is captured in our displays since each party is treated as having its own vectors of experience which embody its code or frame of reference. In addition, Hrushovski's "speech in position" is represented by Box 1: the item concerned is shown as occurring in a larger context, and as nuclear or marginal to the dynamic movement of that larger including context. One also finds points of contact with

Levels of Observer Relationship in Verbal Art   29

? Place in Bailey's biography	Bailey asks Pike to talk at conference	Premargin to presentation	Pike accepts, and begins preparation	Nuclear to talk event	Pike presents talk
(1) ———————————————		(2) ———————————————		(3) ——————————— . . .	
? Perhaps to broaden topics at the conference	Against B's background of linguistics & literature & his knowledge of P's writings	Aimed to inform semiotics audience of use of unit-in-context (tagmeme) in relation to the sympathetic contract	Against linguistic background including postulates about particle, wave, and field (static, dynamic relational unit-in-context)	Presented to inform and interest	In reference to papers given at the conference

A. THE PIKE'S EYE VIEW OF THE TALK

. . . .

B's biography	B asks P	The planning Premargin for the conference	B listens to P's acceptance		
(1) ———————————————		(2) ———————————————		(3) . . . (4) . . . (5) . . .	
cf. A. 1	cf. A. 1	To be able to plan	cf. A. 2		

B. THE BAILEY'S EYE VIEW OF THE TALK

. . . .

		? Biography, place in	Listens to talk		
(1) . . .		(2) ———————————————		(3) . . . (4) . . .	
		? To query ? To enjoy ? To object	With background of personal system		

C. MR. X'S VIEW OF THE TALK (One specific member of the audience)

Figure 2. Three different views (dynamic vectors) of the talk, as seen respectively by Pike, Bailey, and a member of the audience at the 1978 Conference. For the meaning of the four boxes of each unit-in-context (tagmeme), see Figure 1.

Searle (in Giglioli 1972:136-54) where purpose, intention, and function of speech acts between two or more people could be accommodated in Box 3, the role cell.

Tagmemes can also be manipulated to illustrate theories of verbal events which are not illustrated in Figure 2. Hrushovski stated that the listener must construct a frame of reference—an ideology—for the speakers of the text if he is to understand them. In terms of the tagmeme, he is approaching Box 4 from a different direction. The listener must reconstruct the speaker's frame of reference (if it is not known to him) from clues throughout the text and then (metaphorically) place these results as a guess in the appropriate box of the tagmeme.

The combination of Box 3 with Box 4 provides a means to handle the kinds of material discussed under the term 'cooperative principle' by Grice (in Cole and Morgan 1975:41-58—from ms. 1968). According to Grice, each participant in a talk exchange may recognize "a common . . . set of purposes" (Box 3) and contribute to the talk "such as is required . . . by the accepted purpose or directions of the talk exchange" (p. 45). Ultimately, a person's basic social relations, personal characteristics, knowledge, and belief systems (Box 4) govern his or her actions (Box 2) or intentions (Box 3). Similarly, underlying constraints arising from the nature of reason and evidence (Box 4) control conditions for the truth and reasonableness of statements. (Compare the postulates for sincerity and reasonableness conditions in relation to logic, as seen in Gordon and Lakoff, 1971:63-84, reprinted in Cole and Morgan 1975.) Box 3 can also be used to represent the purposes which Larson attributes to various speech acts. According to Larson (1977:5, 116-54), the purpose of narration may be to entertain, relate past events, or covertly teach group values; the purpose of exposition may be to inform about a theme or convey information; the purpose of hortatory text may be to persuade, exhort, ridicule, discipline, command, or overtly teach group values; and the purpose of repartee may be to entertain or affect emotions.

Tagmemes reflect actual human experience. In courts of law, witnesses are asked not only to give an objective view (Box 2) of the events in question, but to state their own intentions (Box 3) and backgrounds (Box 4) as well. Boxes 3 and 4 require us to do the same in our analyses. And Box 1 reflects the way in which an event (Box 2) is scrutinized in courts, not in isolation from other happenings but within larger contexts. Similarly, anthropologists and linguists who seek to understand the intricacies of social relationships and events investigate both the objective and subjective aspects of people within larger contexts. The advantage of tagmemics is that it *systematically* recognizes and notates these features of human experience in a simple but consistent way. And it is therefore a theory which is applicable to poems, music, history, games, and many other happenings.

IV. SPLIT VECTORS AND DUAL ROLE IN THE SPEAKER-LISTENER RELATION

When a single speaker has, from his own viewpoint, two different audiences at the same time, he aims to reach them with different degrees of understanding or with different elements of detail. In such instances there is a *dual purpose*, and each of them is notated in the tagmeme as a component of his *split vector*.

In music, as in speech, two audiences may simultaneously be in view. At the Semiotics Conference, for example, Alan Perlman and Daniel L. Greenblatt discussed the aim of a jazz composer to reach simultaneously an "inner audience" (i.e., an audience with a phrase by phrase structural appreciation of the music) and an "outer audience" whose appreciation of music is more general. (See Figure 3 for my suggestion of a dual-relation representation of this split-level music vector.) Dual simultaneous roles can also be found in the grammatical hierarchy. For instance, in the clause, "I want to be sent home," *I* is simultaneously the actor of *want* and the undergoer (or object) of *to be sent home*. (See Figure 4; also, see Pike and Pike 1977:352-59 for further discussion of dual roles in grammar).

Nucleus (initiative)	Mr. X makes jazz improvisation	Margin (reception)	Audience *i* listens
(1)		(2a)	
(a) Aims at audience *i*	With background of music theory and practice	To follow structure and to enjoy	With background of music theory and practice
(b) Aims at audience *j*		Margin (reception)	Audience *j* listens
		(2b)	
		To enjoy	With general appreciation of jazz

Figure 3. **Split-level Speaker-Audience Relation** in jazz composition (see Perlman and Greenblatt 1980 for data underlying our notation here). The semiotics of music has numerous parallels with that of speech.

Dual roles are evident in different levels of social interaction. An author may himself play a part in a play which he has written. In such an instance he would be the "actor" at different times, in different social relations, once as writer, once as player. Still more complicated would be an instance in which an author writes a play in which he himself is one of the characters, and then plays "himself" in a performance of that play. As Lewis points out, "Shakespeare could, in principle, make himself appear as Author within the play and write a dialogue between Hamlet and himself." In this case, "The 'Shakespeare' within the play would of course be at once Shakespeare and one of Shakespeare's creatures. It would bear some analogy to Incarnation" (1955:277n).

Subject	Pronoun	Predicate (nuclear)	Verb	Object (adjunct)	Passive bitransitive infinitive clause root
(1)		(2)		(3)	
(a) Actor (b) Undergoer of (3)	Subject controls number of predicate Obligatory	Statement	Transitive$_2$ Number controlled by the subject Obligatory	Undergoer of (2)	Obligatory

Figure 4. Dual Role in Grammar; I as simultaneously actor of *want* and undergoer ('patient' or 'logical object') of *to be sent home* (after Pike and Pike 1977:352-59).

V. POSITIVE AND NEGATIVE SYMPATHETIC CONTRACTS IN A PUN EVENT

A. The Pun Itself. I repeat a report of the following event. (The source of the story is unknown to me.)

> A man was walking along a stream, fishing. He came to a sign beside the brook. He read it aloud: "[dont fĭš hir]." He replied, "I don't know," and went on fishing.

This sign, of course, was spelled "here," but the fisherman pretended that it was spelled "hear" and that it was a question.

B. External and Internal Levels of Social Interaction in Relation to the Pun

1) The first level of social interaction relates the author of the joke to his original audience (both unknown to me).

2) The second level of social interaction relates me to the readers of my book on the intonation of American English (1945:45-46) where this pun is quoted.

3) A third level of social interaction relates me to the audience at the Semiotics Conference 33 years later.

4) Internal to the joke itself is the relation between the writer of the sign and potential poachers of the fish in the stream.

5) Also internal to the joke is the relation of this particular fisherman to some other imaginary audience—either himself speaking to himself or to some generalized potential listeners.

C. Purpose and Cohesion on these Levels of Social Interaction.

To formalize these five levels (see Figure 5), we must make explicit the sympathetic contracts which implicitly exist between the participants. We do so by examining the background beliefs of the participants, the sincerity and truth of their beliefs, and any other background materials which control or are controlled by the events (Box 4). Similarly, we evaluate the purpose or reason for these events (Box 3) in order to have fuller data for our formalization. If these factors are unknown to us, we must either guess or confess our ignorance.

For the first of these interactions (Figure 5A—the relation of the author of the joke to his initial audience), we may assume that the author's purpose was to surprise and please his audience with the pun, and that this purpose was coherent with a belief that some people enjoy puns. Similarly, we may assume that the purpose of the listener was to understand or to "make sense" of what the speaker was saying. In terms of the sympathetic contract, the listener had to believe that the speaker was trying to make sense. Note, however, that a person can deliberately refuse to fulfill his part of the sympathetic contract, and this refusal becomes part of the technical description of the material. It shows up as the *negative* fulfillment of cohesion relations in Box 4 of the appropriate tagmeme of the formula.

In 1945 (Figure 5B), the participants and relationships were different. My purpose was to use the joke to illustrate the fact that a statement and a question can have identical intonation under appropriate circumstances. The pun in this joke does not work unless the intonation of the question is homophonous with that of the statement; the question must be read with a falling intonation on *hear*—like a statement—or the audience will *expect* the fisherman's reply and the pun will fail.

34 Tagmemics, Discourse, and Verbal Art

? Context unknown	? Author unknown	? Context unknown	? Audience unknown, listens
(1)		(2)	
To surprise and please the audience	With belief that hearer will be puzzled by "hearing" wrong part of the pun	First, to attempt to find an apparent meaning— then, enjoy the joke	Coherent with assumption that author intends sense— but that authors sometimes joke

A. EXPERIENCE VECTOR OF ORIGINAL WRITER (of the Fish Joke)

As section of textbook of 1945	Pike writes with technical analysis	? Context of use unknown (unless student assignment)	Read by audience
(1)		(2)	
To illustrate that intonation is not determined by grammar	Coherent with belief that *any* intonation pattern can be used for question	To advance in understanding the nature and meaning of intonation	With tentative acceptance of the value of intonation study to linguistics— or of the need to understand Pikes view

B. EXPERIENCE VECTOR OF PIKE 1945

Part of semiotics conference	Joke told and analyzed by Pike	Middle illustration (Margin)	Audience listens
(1)		(2)	
To illustrate levels of social relations	With hierarchical theory	To get acquainted with the theory	With positive —or negative— reaction in relation to semiotics

C. PIKE'S VECTOR 1978

Levels of Observer Relationship in Verbal Art 35

? Prior loss of fish	Land owner posts sign
(1)	
To keep people from fishing there	Belief in private property—and in peoples' obedience to the law

D. FARMER'S VECTOR

Nucleus of action	Fisherman reads aloud (with falling intonation pattern)	Post nuclear action	Continues fishing
(1)		(2)	
To pretend misunderstanding	Coherent with belief in private property Negative coherence with intent of sign	To catch fish ? To spite owner ? To enjoy the joke	Cf. (1), Box 4 Coherent with pretense of having fulfilled a request

E. FISHERMAN'S VECTOR

Figure 5. Different Dynamic Experience Vectors (referential sequence) in the fishing joke.

Cohesive with the purpose of illustrating intonation I had to have the conviction that intonation in American English does not always differentiate explicitly between question and statement, and that context sometimes has to force the interpretation one way or the other (Pike 1945:163-68). For the sympathetic contract to work in this relationship, the purpose of the readers had to be to try to understand the particular theory of intonation I was propounding; and cohesive with that there had to be some kind of belief—deeply accepted or temporarily adopted—that intonation might have broader ranges of usage and more intricate structures than the readers had previously suspected.

In the 1978 Conference (Figure 5D), the purposes of the speaker (me) and the listeners were different. I was using the joke to illustrate the fact that a social exchange occurs with different levels of relationship in an n-dimensional field. Cohesive with this presentation was the underlying belief that tagmemic analysis can be extended to formalize such relationships. I was assuming that the audience included at least some persons who were listening in order to find out what I consider these relationships to be, and that this material would be cohesive with their broader interests in semiotics.

In the pun (Figure 5D) the farmer who made the sign—in fact or in fiction—wished to keep persons from fishing in his stream, and this was probably coherent with his belief in the rights of private property. Most readers of his sign would presumably want to avoid being fined or jailed for infringing on his property rights, and this desire would be coherent with their knowledge of the law.

The fisherman who came along in this fictional situation (Figure 5E) had yet a different purpose—he wanted to fish. Cohesive with his desire to fish, however, was his belief in private property rights, and his desire to avoid getting into trouble with the law. In order to avoid the interdiction preventing him from fishing, he pretended that the sign did not forbid him to fish (but asked him a question); with this interpretation, the sign did not imply that he would get into trouble if he were challenged for fishing near the sign. the fisherman's perspective provides an example of negative cohesion with the sympathetic contract implicit in communication. The fisherman was expected to read the sign as the writer intended it to be read, i.e., as a warning. Instead, he deliberately flouted the intent of the writer by ignoring its unambiguous spelling and reading it aloud with an intonation which permitted an interpretation contrary to the intent of the writer. The fact that he did this must have been cohesive with a conviction that he could "get away with it," or talk himself out of any penalty by claiming that he had read the sign and responded to it in an "appropriate" way (i.e., by answering the question it asked).

At the Semiotics Conference, Seymour Chatman based his analysis of codes of verisimilitude on a six-participant view of a narration, reminiscent of our levels in the treatment of the pun. His first participant (the real narrator) and his last reader (the real reader) are entirely compatible with my own view of text-makers and text-interpreters as illustrated in this discussion. Similarly, his categories of implied author and reader could be related to the original formulator of the joke and that audience. His story participants are analogous to the farmer and poacher in the pun, and his assertion that people must develop a 'code' or universe of discourse against which the text makes sense is related to Box 4—the cohesion cell—of our referential hierarchy.

Nicolas Ruwet suggested at the Conference that sometimes we do not find the expected parallelisms on the surface of poems, but that an analysis of syntactic, intonational, and other levels of the poem will sometimes reveal parallelisms. Our discussion of this pun also suggests the need for study of parallelisms across hierarchical levels.

Our work is also related to John Blacking's presentation of research into ethnomusicology at the Conference. In his discussion of the "meaning" of music Blacking insisted that there is a need for treating seriously the judgments of ordinary nonspecialist members of the community. Different perceptions of a sonata by composer, performer, listener, and analyst all become part of the sonata. Likewise, for speech, the different perceptual approaches (*emic*—see Pike 1967) and varying audiences enter into our linguistic analysis.

VI. A POEM PUN WITH HEAR/HERE

We have shown how various levels of social interaction can be involved in a simple pun. Looking at the pun in the context of a poem (in Pike 1971b:104), we find an even more complex interlocking of relationships among people telling the story.

A. **The Story and the Poem.** The poem is based on a story composed of five episodes:
  (*a*) A mob comes with swords and clubs to arrest Jesus.
  (*b*) Peter pulls out his sword and chops off one of Malchus' ears.
  (*c*) Jesus says that sword play is neither desirable nor necessary.
  (*d*) Jesus touches Malchus' ear and heals it.
  (*e*) The disciples flee.

The poem itself, as published, is comprised of two imagined conversational interchanges: one between Malchus and Peter, and the other between Jesus and Malchus (see Figure 6).

HEAR!

"Hey! How can I hear?
You chopped my ear off!
Is it a cap to doff?"

"Sorry.
Take it back.
Here!"

Figure 6. Poem (from Pike 1971b:104).

B. Levels of Reporting the Event.

1. Matthew, Mark, Luke, and John each gave a written report of this event. Each one tells the story a different way, and each has a different vector of experience and a different purpose in relating the event. For example, John (18:8-12) records that the ear which Peter cut off was the right one and that the person injured was Malchus; but he does not mention the healing of the ear. Matthew (26:47-51) reports Jesus' statement that supernatural help would have come if called for, but that it was not appropriate. Mark (14:47-50) tells about the ear being cut off and adds that one of Jesus' friends, presumably himself, ran away naked when someone grabbed onto his garment as he fled. Luke (22:48-54) mentions that Jesus touched the ear and restored it. In spite of the differences in their reports, the disciples presumably shared certain purposes (Box 3): to give a narrative of the last days of their discipleship; to show Jesus' calmness and gentleness of spirit; and to suggest events that transcend the violence of our human world. Each of them placed this event in a marginal slot (Box 1) leading up to a climax in the life of the chief character.

2. Another order of social interaction occurred when the Aramaic conversational component of the original event was translated into the Greek narrative. Presumably, the purpose of the translator was to reach a larger audience, and this purpose was coherent with the fact that Greek was then the lingua franca of that part of the world. In addition, the translator must have had some concept of truth in reporting, and cohesive with this there must have been some kind of translation theory specifying which of the grammatical features and lexical senses had to be preserved.

3. Much more accessible to us is the stage of translation from Greek to English. With the large number of different translations—some of them made by people still living—we have a better opportunity to discuss changes in translation in relation to particular audiences. But this level is beyond the scope of this paper.

4. More remote from the actual event is my writing of the poem and the audience I was hoping to reach while doing so. The humor in the published poem would hardly have been appropriate at the time of the action. The poem must be treated as conversation pretended in retrospect, used to lighten up the report of what must have been a grim scene. This lightness is achieved not only by the pun of *hear/here,* but by the metaphor of *cap* (hat) for *ear* which is reinforced by the lexical meaning of *doff* 'to take off or lift up the hat.' The rhyming of *off* and *doff*, in addition to other characteristics of phonology—for instance, intonation and voice quality—also contributes to the mood of the poem.

Beyond simple grammar, the "gap" after the third line (or the "fulcrum" or "silence") is important to the poem, indicating an abrupt change of speaker-audience relation as well as a sharp change (when read aloud) in voice quality and phonological dynamics. Ciardi emphasizes that this component is present in any effective poem (1959:1002, 1004, 1007).

5. At the Conference I used this poem in a radically different context. My purpose in using it was to illustrate levels of relationship in reported social events and to help the audience understand some of my current interests in linguistic structure which relate to a broader interest in semiotics.

C. Unit-in-Context Representation of Participants of the Event.

So far, I have emphasized the events of writing, listening, or reacting. I have implied that the attitudes of participants influence their reaction to events and their motivation in events. Now, however, I will focus directly on the participants themselves and show that they can be viewed or analyzed within the same frame of reference that I have been using for events. Specifically, for Box 1 (slot) I ask how the participant fits into a larger social structure. For Box 2 (class or set of classes) I ask that the specific participant (or set of participants) be labelled or identified by a word, a phrase, or a set of paraphrases. For instance, a sequence of paraphrases of *coyote* are found in a story about a coyote and a rabbit (Pike and Pike 1977:375-376): the rabbit calls the coyote *coyote, uncle,* or *you* when speaking to him; the coyote refers to himself as *I* when speaking to the rabbit; and the narrator of the folk tale sometimes refers to the coyote as *animal.* These would be specified in Box 2. Members of a paraphrase set do not have to be single words; they can be phrases or descriptive clauses or even paragraphs (e.g., *the animal who is the villain, the one who is deceived into thinking that the reflection of the moon is the cheese,* etc.).

In Box 3 the participant's role and purpose are specified. Note that the perspective of the person describing the participant influences the content of this box. When we call the coyote *villain*, we are referring to the general judgment of the community as a whole. If we were giving the coyote's own vector, Box 3 would not include *villain* as his role since the coyote views himself differently. Hence, even the role of the participant is cohesive with someone's universe of discourse, belief system, or evaluative attitude (Box 4). In general, unless otherwise specified, the contents of Box 3 will agree with the judgment of the narrator or describer of the event. If the narrator changes, the analysis of the event will change, and the new narrator's evaluation of the purposes of an event and the role of the participants will be specified in Box 3. The narrator's evaluation of specific personal characteristics of the participants—such as honesty, intelligence, or social adaptability—are placed in Box 4.

The sympathetic contract reflects the underlying belief systems which make a poem acceptable or unacceptable to a reader and affects the way an event will be reported by two observers who have differing ideologies. No report of an event can be neutral when it includes the recording of purposes (Box 3) and background understandings (Box 4) in addition to the objective facts (Box 2). Yet without the recording of purpose and intent, an event is not fully reported. In some cases, even "objective" reports (e.g., films of an event) are subject to the biases of the reporter (e.g., the cameraman and editor). The reporter's biases, ideology, belief system, and experience (Box 4) are sometimes reflected in the parts of the event (Box 2) he chooses to present in the movie.

My report in the poem of the story of Malchus' ear reflects some of my biases. Within this constraint, therefore, and specifically in relation to the fact that I am the author of the poem being discussed, I will record some of my judgments about the participants.

Figure 7 (A) shows the notation for Peter (Box 2) who was the one who chopped off the ear. He is in the nuclear group of three (of the twelve) disciples (Box 1); the leader of the group as a whole (Box 3); and impulsive in character (Box 4).

A.		
	Among the inner three	Peter The one who chopped the ear off
	Leader of the twelve disciples	Impulsive

B.		
	At the nucleus of the movement	Jesus
	(a) Founder of movement (b) Hero (viewpoint of the Gospels) (c) Villain (view of the mob)	(a) Calm under pressure (b) In control of followers (c) With healing powers

Figure 7. Participants (Peter and Jesus) shown via notation of unit-in-context on participant level of the hierarchy.

When we earlier showed dual role (in Figure 3), it was in relation to the intent of a speaker aiming at different parts of his audiences. Figure 7 (B) illustrates a different kind of dual role in reference to Jesus: the different evaluations of him (or roles attributed to him) by onlookers. In this instance, disciples and mob perhaps agreed on his role as founder of the movement; but presumably disagreed as to his role as hero or villain. A full description of an event includes not only the dynamic vectors of experience for each actor, but evaluations of the actors from different viewpoints.

VII. GRAMMATICAL VERSUS REFERENTIAL ANALOGUES WITHIN PAIRED HIERARCHIES

I mentioned in Section II that there are differences between the grammatical and referential hierarchies. There are also parallels between the two hierarchies (see Figure 8). For instance, in grammar there is clear difference of hierarchical level between an independent clause (or a sentence composed of clauses) and a word (or a phrase composed of words). There is a certain kind of *isolability* which an (independent) clause and sentence have which is quite different from the isolability of a word or phrase under ordinary conditions of discourse. An independent clause (or sentence) can initiate a discussion, making an affirmation (or question or command). A single word or phrase usually does not comprise such an isolated element (except when a word by itself comprises a clause, as in some imperatives such as *Come!*). Affirmations (or propositions) normally relate words or phrases.

Analogously, in the referential hierarchy an *event* or happening is isolable in description. On the other hand, to participants (such as persons or animals) or to such other *identity* elements (using a term of Jones 1977:108-109) as props (e.g., tables, mountains, streets, actions not affirmed), we assign the status of item. Items must be related by events, just as words are related by propositions.

There are intriguing semiotic parallels between speech and music. At the Semiotics Conference, Allan Keiler presented a paper in which he treated musical 'constituency' (hierarchically syntagmatic and perhaps analogous to our grammatical hierarchy) and music 'grouping' (perhaps analogous to the referential hierarchy) as quite distinct from each other. Blacking insisted that nonmusical factors—the way an item is *used* and defined by ordinary people—are essential to the adequate analysis of artistic *processes*, a chief concern of the semiotician of music. It seems to me that Blacking makes social interaction the chief entrance point for the analysis of music as a form-meaning *composite* (not music as mere form). Social interaction is also the entrance point for the analysis of the grammatical hierarchy in our approach to language (Pike and Pike 1977:22-23).

GRAMMMATICAL	REFERENTIAL
Social interaction seen in classes of dialogue exchange or in conversation	Performative interaction seen in speech acts
Theme development seen in classes of paragraph or monologue	Network of events seen in story (or "script"), description, or set of instructions
Proposition or assertion seen in classes of clause or sentence	Purpose or explanation seen in dynamic experience or static description
Term seen as classes of word or phrase	Identities seen as participants, props, settings, or groups thereof
Lexical package as a form-meaning composite (cf. the "sign") seen as classes of morphemes and morpheme clusters	Culturally relevant form-plus-"meaning" elements seen as characteristics of participants, props, settings, or identities

Figure 8. Some potential analogues between classes of units of the grammatical and referential analogues (cf. Pike and Pike 1977: 24-26, 364-85, and Jones 1977:109-13).

We have been treating grammatical ordering as linear, and referential ordering as (often) chronological. At the Conference, Judith Becker warned that Westerners are biased in favor of the apparent 'naturalness' of chronology—while the Javanese treat simultaneity as a 'natural' basis for coherence. It is unclear how this alternative basic frame of reference may be added to our system; eventually, however, we must include the total network of relations perceived by whatever observer.

VIII. PHONOLOGICAL HIERARCHY IN THE POEM

Many people assume that someone other than its author will do a better job of reading a poem. From the point of view of this discussion, there can be no quarrel with this opinion, (if someone believes it to be true). It merely forces us to specify another level of social interaction: the interaction of reader of the poem with the listener to the poem. In the cohesion cell specifying the reaction or character of a particular listener, it must be stated that that person prefers the oral interpretation of performers who are not authors. My opinion is, however, quite different. Our tradition has encouraged the assumption that a poem has been fully created in written form; that the poet's task is finished when he has the words in English orthography. My own view is that the poet should be allowed to say what he means, and that part of what he means can be carried by the pitch of the voice and by voice quality. Poets often use capital letters, dashes, or arrangements in various lines to affect the way the poem will be read. I think poets should be encouraged to add more explicit pitch and voice quality indications to the poem, and I have argued and illustrated this point elsewhere (Pike 1971a; voice quality components are also illustrated extensively in a poem by Vachel Lindsay, "The Congo," in Ciardi 1959:938-41). The implication is that poets need to be trained to be sensitive to meanings of intonation, just as they are currently trained to be sensitive to the meaning of words. It could take many years—and a different set of poets—to utilize creatively the resources of English in this way.

In Figure 9 I have added intonation to the poem shown without it in Figure 6. Note that the extra high (shown by the line substantially above the letters in line 2) suggests the intensity of surprise. Each of the pitches falling from a stress mark calls attention to that particular element. The low pitch rising to high on *doff* (line 4) indicates deliberateness followed by incompleteness—implying protest, or something yet to come (in this particular context, a question). The repeated mid-low characteristic in lines 5-7 gives the flavor of 'detachedness,' or relaxed abstraction—implying in this context a kind of soothing quality in the face of the radical upset of the scene. The extra high non-stressed syllable sequence in line 4 (*is it a*) leads to a very sharp contrast with a low stress (on *cap*). The double slash (at the end of lines 1, 4, 5) indicates a kind of finality, a lower pitch and fade of intensity. The single slash (end of lines 2, 3) implies that the present line flows into the next without a break. The ligatures in *take it back* (line 6) indicate a kind of unifying effect. The use of such devices becomes effective if and only if the poet and the audience are both sensitive to the differences they suggest, and if the poet uses them in an artistic way. (For the general attitudinal meanings to these intonation types, see the extensive discussion in Pike 1945).

Other phonological aspects of the poem are also important. For instance, the change in voice quality to a relaxed soothing tone in the last line; the rhyme of *off* with *doff*; the phonological homonymity of *hear* and *here*; and the phonological similarity of *hear* and *ear*. The crescendo building to *doff* adds to the protest; the repeated aspiration

44 Tagmemics, Discourse, and Verbal Art

(the sound *h*) in the first line gives a kind of breathy quality which could suggest Malchus' distress (catching his breath). Phonology intersects with the grammatical and referential hierarchies to carry the total impact of the poem, and these three are simultaneously manifested by the lexical elements.

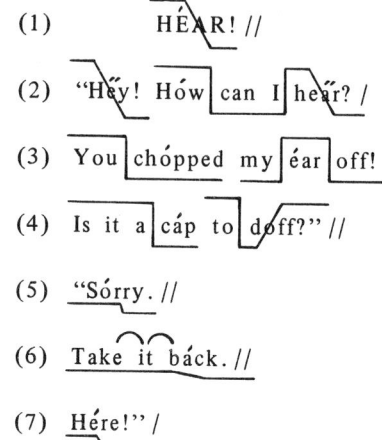

Figure 9. **The poem** of Figure 6, marked for intonation, stress, and pause. Mid tone is directly below the letters; high tone directly above them; low and extra high respectively substantially below or above. Stress is marked with acute accent; extra stress as double. Concluding pause is signalled by double slash; a tentative pause by single slash; a rhythm break with grave mark; unitizing with ligature.

Poets may want to read their poems in different ways, at different times (and their interpreters may choose to do likewise). What then? A poem may have two or more variants with different but related messages carried not by its words but by intonation and voice quality. I believe that poets should be encouraged to record as many of variations as they find interesting, true, or beautiful.

Figure 10 illustrates the quite different meanings that can result from a change in intonation and voice quality. Two versions of one verse of a poem—"How can I Remember (When I Forget)?"—are displayed (with the words—but not the intonation marking—from Pike and Stephen Pike 1977:43; see also pp. 16 and 30 for two poems marked for intonation). Variant A is intended to show unhappiness and regret at an oversight; Variant B is designed to show deep sarcasm.

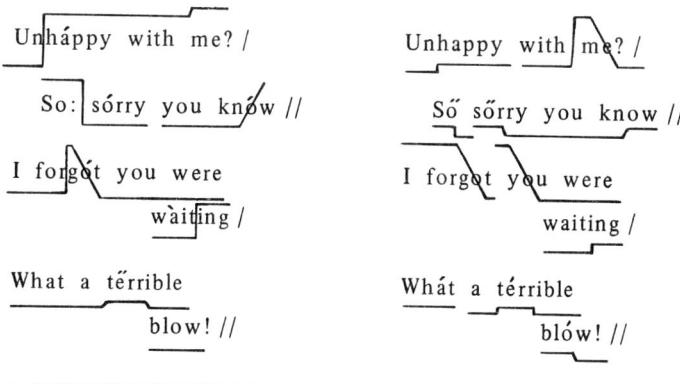

A. WITH DEEP GENUINE REGRET   B. WITH SARCASM

Figure 10. A Verse from "How can I remember (when I forget)" (from Pike and Stephen Pike 1977:43) showing two intonational variants. High and mid pitches are just above and just below the letters; extra high and low are further above and further below.

In additon to intonation and voice quality, a class of phonemes may serve as a feature of a phonological unit-in-context, just as a class of words can serve as a feature of a grammatical tagmeme. In Figure 11 a class of consonants (Box 2) serves as marginal to the syllable (Box 1); these consonants help to identify lexical units (Box 3) and belong to a system of sounds in which distinctive features make up a system of contrastive characteristics (Box 4).

(Slot) Before or after nucleus	(Class) Consonant class (C = p/t/k; b/d/g . . .)
(Role) Contributing to contrastive or identificational function of lexical units	(Cohesion) Belongs to a system of sounds within a distinctive-feature matrix—controls some in adjacent sounds—and in part controlled by them

Figure 11. A phonological unit-in-context.

Another way in which the phonological hierarchy parallels the grammatical and referential ones is in its isolable items. In Figure 9 we indicated that some grammatical and referential items were more isolable than others, and the same is true of phonological items. Phonological items which are unpronounceable in isolation are nonisolable. Most of the consonants are completely unpronounceable in isolation (i.e., without using an adjoining vowel to make up a "naming" syllable for the sound). It may take considerable practice and effort before a beginning student of phonetics can pronounce one after another of the isolated sounds of a sentence. It is only with the syllable or with a group of syllables or a rhythm (stress) group that isolation comes easily, and hence the syllable or stress group has special status, analogous to the clause or sentence or event.

On the highest level of social interchange, a *phonological contract* may be observed. A person asking a question in a very rapid voice, with evidence of urgency, may be answered in a more rapid voice than would otherwise be expected; and in some instances the choice of dialect pronunciation may elicit a comparable reply.

IX. WHEN DO YOU STOP?

One of the chief difficulties with our view of the referential hierarchy is that you can go on and on, deeper and deeper into the concepts and frames of reference involved. Just when do you decide to stop in the analysis? When the analyst-observer reaches the depth of detail which interests him or satisfies his purposes, he stops. A different person, with different purposes or different experiences (e.g., literary critic or medical person) would ask different questions and seek different answers.

When different investigators quiz various people about different phases of an event, different personal vectors of interest and competence are encountered, and the details are consequently organized in different ways. Sometimes the informants are unable to give us answers, and at that point we either deduce—and guess—or we stop. In many historical investigations, no informants are available and we need to stop long before we are satisfied—and our guesses remain permanently different and unanswerable.

In this article I have moved from the discussion of general principles of unit, hierarchy, context, and perspective, to a presentation of the tagmeme: a unit-in-context which utilizes well-known elements, but combines them in such a way that the notation can be applied to pun and poem, to words and pitch, to participant and event, to purpose and grammar. This synthesis is to me an exciting one since it opens the door to further attempts to unify science and literature.

Grammar versus Reference in the Analysis of Discourse

For many decades linguists limited their analysis of language to the structure of words. In the past two decades, they expanded their investigation to include the analysis of larger units: phrases, clauses and sentences. Recently, however, linguists have begun an inquiry into the structure of total discourse. This fortunate development brings them into closer relation with scholars interested in the formal structure of literature. However, a major constraint characterizes the work of many of these linguists: they have no effective means of dealing with the concept of reference. They either treat it as a part of grammar, ignore it altogether, or make it too abstract. In this essay, I will show why it is necessary for a theory of language to incorporate a referential hierarchy distinct from a grammatical hierarchy, and I will propose some directions for the formal representation of a referential hierarchy.

I. THE STRUCTURE OF A HAPPENING VERSUS THE STRUCTURE OF TELLING ABOUT THAT HAPPENING

Americans beginning to study French often have difficulty learning to use liaison and elision properly. From a tagmemic perspective, the problem arises because the phonological and grammatical hierarchies in French are not isomorphic, as they more often are in English. Often

---

[1] An earlier version of this paper was prepared for *Perspectives dans l'analyse du discours, Publications conjointes de l'Institut de Linguitique Appliquee de L'Universite d'Abidjan et de la Société Internationale de Linguistique,* (Ed. Thomas Bearth).

in French the final consonant of a morpheme or word is pronounced as a part of the first syllable of the next morpheme or word. As a result, morphological and phonological boundaries are not coterminous. Consider, for example, *me.s a.mis* 'my friends,' where the periods show syllable division and the space between *s* and *a* a word boundary. Examples of this type are abundant and provide evidence of the need to treat phonological and grammatical hierarchies separately.

Similar arguments may be provided to show that grammar and reference structures are sometimes not isomorphic and therefore must be treated separately in theory and analysis. By taking an event and recounting it several different ways, we can illustrate this idea. An event and its report may be structured quite similarly in a simple case; in a complex situation they must be structured very differently. Although several things can occur simultaneously, several things cannot be said simultaneously. We can show this experimentally. Figure 1 is a matrix of labelled rows and columns, with combined symbols in the cells at the point of intersection of row and column. It has been constructed to represent the following story, with the rows representing the activity of the different characters, and the columns representing roughly identifiable time equivalences.

	1	2	3	4
A:	A1	A2	A3	A4
B:	B1	B2	B3	B4
C:	C1	C2	C3	C4

Figure 1. An arbitrary set of rows and columns, intersecting in the labelled cells of the matrix.

(A1)   Abe went downtown to go to work.
  (A2)   He met Bill.
  (A3)   They had lunch together.
  (A4a) Clara came past. (A4b) Abe invited her to join them, (A4c) but she refused, saying that she did not feel well.
(B1) Meanwhile, Bill had left his office on an errand into the city center.
  (B2)   He met Abe.
  (B3)   They had lunch together.
  (B4a) While they were eating, Clara came past (B4b) and was invited to join them, (B4c) but she refused.

(C1) It so happened that Clara also had gone downtown
    (C2)   shopping
    (C3)   for some time.
    (C4a)   Suddenly she glanced up—and there was her friend Abe, eating with his friend Bill (whom she detested). (C4b) They invited her to join them, (C4c) but she said that she was ill since she didn't want to eat with Bill.

The order of this telling is illustrated in Figure 2. Starting at the top of the matrix, the story works down from the left to right within each row. Each participant is discussed separately, but the times overlap from row to row. Although subevents A1, B1, and C1 happened more or less at the same time, they are discussed sequentially. The *telling* sequence for each separate (but simultaneous) participant action is given chronologically—subevent 1 (of Column 1) happened before subevent 2, which occurred before subevent 3.

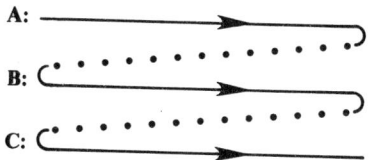

Figure 2. **Order** of the first telling of the story, with the actions (subevents) of each participant treated separately.

The telling of this event (in English) can start at different points. For example, we can begin in a complex way with all of Column 4, and then move back separately in sequence to Rows A, B, and C. This order gives the effect of a "flashback." We diagram this pattern in Figure 3 and retell the story in that order.

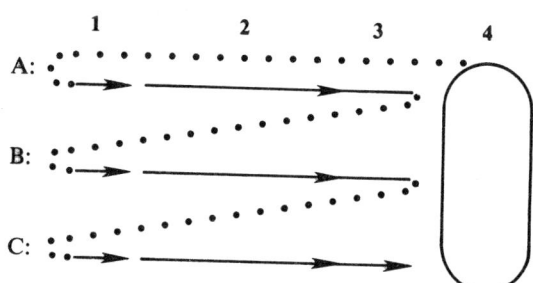

Figure 3. **A flashback**, with the last part of the story told first. It starts with Column 4 as a whole, then moves to Row A, to B, to C.

(A4, B4, C4) What an awkward coincidence that was!
  (C4a)   Clara glanced up
  (A4a, B4a, C4a) as she walked past a table at a sidewalk restaurant.
  (A4b, C4b) There sat her close friend Abe, eating with that detested Bill.
  (A4b)   What could they do? Abe invited her to join them.
  (B4b)   (Bill presumably grunted his agreement "politely"— Although I am not quite sure how.)
  (C4c)   And what could *she* do? She told a white lie, pleading off for illness, and passed on.
(A1) The problem had arisen when Abe went to work downtown.
  (A2)   Meeting Bill,
  (A3)   he stopped to lunch with him—
(E1) a meeting made possible by the earlier coincidence that Bill had left his office
  (B2)   for an errand in the city, where the meeting occurred.
  (B3)   So they had lunch together,
(C1) not dreaming that Clara would be coming downtown
  (C2)   to shop
  (C3)   for a while,
  (C4)   and then wander past their table
(A4, B4, C4) and see them!

This telling order differs quite strikingly from the happening order. If retellings are to preserve the original meaning (i.e., if they are to "tell the same story"), English grammar requires that signals (or combinations of signals) be added to orient the listener. In this particular retelling, many such signals occur: for example, "The problem had arisen" (A1) signals that the narrator is going to back up to an earlier time, as does "made possible by the earlier coincidence" (B1).

A telling order which works through the chart down the columns, instead of across the rows, captures the simultaneity of the subevents (see Figure 4).

  (A1)   Abe, (B1) Bill, and (C1) Clara had all gone downtown.
    (A2, B2, C2) Bill and Abe met while Clara was shopping.
    (C3, A3, B3) While Abe and Bill were eating, Clara wandered past.
    (A4, B4, C4) Although invited to join them, she refused.

Grammar vs. Reference in the Analysis of Discourse 51

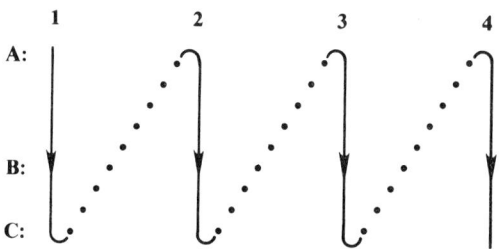

Figure 4. Simultaneity attempted by using grammatical forms in which components of subevents can be grouped acceptably.

Figure 5 diagrams a linking of the events of Row A. The chaining involves partial repetition of one item as an introduction to the next.

(A1) Abe went to work. After he went to work
  (A2)   he met Bill. Having met Bill,
  (A3)   they ate together.

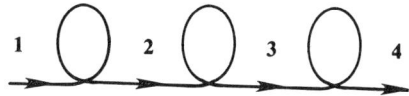

Figure 5. Chaining — the partial repetition of a form as an entry into the next form.

The repetition of the telling does *not* imply that the event happened twice. This is powerful evidence that telling structures and happening structures are not the same. [See Longacre 1968: Vol. 1, Part 2, 1.1 for an illustration of this pattern used in the Philippines; and Wise 1971: 166-67 for the theoretical implication that this kind of duplication forces a difference between the telling form (her 'G-paragraph') and the happening form (her 'L-paragraph'). The terminology is different from ours, but the principles are related.]

Figure 6 diagrams a telling order which begins with one part of the happening and adds successive parts to the original statement:

(A1) Abe went.
  (A1-2) He went to town.
  (A1-2-3-4) He went to town and met Bill and ate with him.

Alternatively, the succession could have points added without the whole being repeated in an overlay (cf. Grimes 1972:292-97):

(A1) Abe went to his work. He went to town.

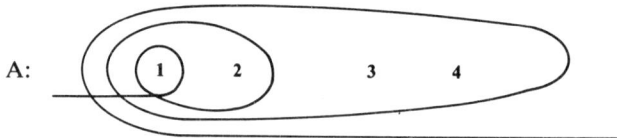

Figure 6. **The development** of a statement by successively added material.

Javanese stories typically place an emphasis on coincidence (cf. reference in Pike and Pike 1977:270-71 to Becker). This story may be reordered to do the same (see Figure 7).

(A4, B4, C4) They met! How annoying.
    C4c)   Clara had been trying to avoid Bill for weeks.
    (A1)   But Abe went downtown, and
    (E1)   Bill did too—
(A2, B2) The two of them met, and
(A3, B3) lunched together.
(C4a, A3, B3, B4a) Clara "just happened" to pass by as they
    were eating . . .
(A4, B4, C4) Could it have been coincidental? Or was it somehow
    "meant to be"? She rejected the idea.

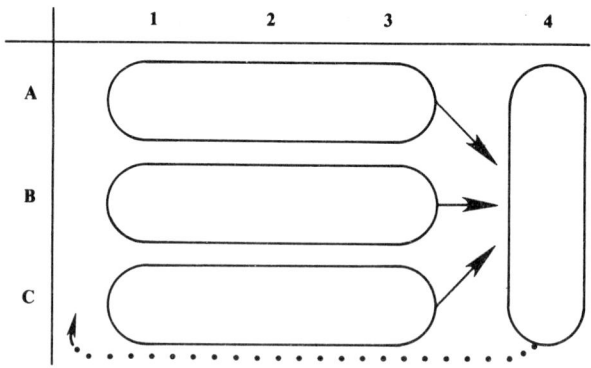

Figure 7. **Coincidence**—This diagram suggests that focus is on the meeting (Column 4).

In the European tradition, writers of narrative often try to present their material in some kind of temporal progression. As illustrated above, however, simultaneities resist simple progressions, and other telling techniques must be employed. Usually the narrator either tells a complete subevent first (Figure 2), tells an analogous part of each subevent in a single section (Figure 4), or uses a combination of these strategies.

Sometimes the telling order of an event appears to the reader to be completely random, though in most cases the order is carefully planned to give a special aesthetic result. With appropriate grammatical clues, a random telling order becomes feasible in English. Figure 8 and the following variant of our story demonstrates this idea. The order was randomly chosen by me with no prior plan (i.e., no semantic or structural intent).

(C4c) Clara made up a flimsy excuse.
(B2-A2) It seems that Bill and Abe had met,
(C1-2-3) and Clara, who had gone downtown shopping for a while,
(C4a, B4a, A4a) ran into them—a regretable coincidence since she detested Bill.
(A3-B3) These two men were having lunch together,
(A1) (since Abe was downtown for work)
(A4b, B4b, C4b) and Abe invited Clara to join them.
(B1) Bill, who had left his office on an errand,
(B2-3) and had met Abe, and joined him for lunch,
(A4c, B4c, C4c) was someone Clara didn't want to eat with. So she refused to join them
(C4a) when she passed by the sidewalk restaurant
(A3-B3) where they were.

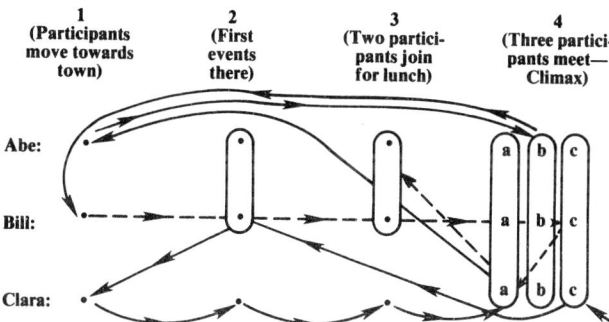

Figure 8. A somewhat **random order** of filling in the matrix. It results in highlighting Clara's refusal. Begin with C4c; follow the path indicated by the arrows; end with third contact with A3-B3. (A second or third contact is shown by broken lines.(When two or three points are circled, they are treated as "same"—an inclusive multiple-point in the path—for the immediate story-telling purpose.

Figure 8 shows how each cell in the matrix was used in this story sequence. Since none of the information was left out, and appropriate grammatical clues were given, the reader can reconstruct the entire referential set of relationships.

Much of the material in a report has to do with the actual happening and is given in a basic event sequence. Other material in the report gives supplementary information concerning the situation, prior happenings, or characteristics of persons. Often the background material is "out of order"—inserted into the middle of the event stream. And often this information is put into parentheses, modifying clauses, or other devices. One bit of background information was parenthetically mentioned in the initial story in C4a: *whom she detested*. If the details of our chart had been chronological at that point, this phrase would have been given a position *before* any of the subevents listed. The analyst's careful chronological charting of events often helps to reveal some of the underlying structure by forcing some of the background information to a position early in the chart where it would not have seemed appropriate in a classical outline. (For a sample chart, see Pike and Pike 1977:272-74, concerning data on Berik of Irian Jaya collected by Westrum; for a different way of handling background, see the Thurman chart in Grimes 1975:83-87.)

We have not come close to exhausting the possibilities of telling this story in structurally different ways. Among the most important source of difference is observer perspective. Different people who report an event and feel differently about it may show differences in the way they tell the story. Observer differences we treat as referentially different.

Figure 9 places the observer-reporter outside the story. The reporter can react to the story, which he has heard and now retells, with belief, anger, annoyance, humor, or "remoteness"—noncommittal to its factualness or relevance. Here, the speaker delights in gossiping about someone else's misfortune. Items added by that observer are placed in brackets.

(0) [Would you ever believe it! I just heard it myself.]
(C2-3 and AB4) That two-faced Clara, who had in fact been downtown for some time, [and must have been hungry,]
(C4c) cut Bill (that detestable jerk!).
(C4a) She saw him eating with her [adorable boy-] friend Abe.
(C4a) Abe is Bill's friend too, [believe it or not—oh boy! what a situation].
(ABC4c) Anyway, Clara refused even to sit at the table with them (pretending she was sick!).

(C4c) Abe urged her to—
(ABC4b) and Bill [kind of grunted "politely," "Oh yes, do join us!"]
(AB2-3) Of course you realize that both Abe and Bill had met and [naturally]—(C4a) as friends, started to lunch together, [not dreaming that Clara might come by!].
(0) [So there is a pretty story!]
(ABC1-3) Each of them had gone downtown for work or on errands of some kind, and had no idea that the other two would be there.
(0) [Life *does* have its amusing coincidences. "Boy meets girl"—Oh yeah? And how!]

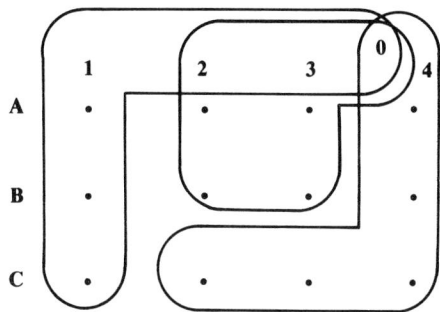

Figure 9. A particular observer (0) recounts the story from a particular perspective with a particular attitude. Each subevent described by him may be "infected" by his evaluation, belief system, experience and intent for telling. Replacement of speaker (or of audience) changes the referential structure.

If grammatical and referential structures may overlap (even to the point of isomorphism at times), how can they be differentiated and represented formally? To this question we now turn.

II. NOTATION FOR REFERENCE VERSUS GRAMMAR VIA FOUR-CELLED UNIT-IN-CONTEXT

It should now be clear, I think, that referential constants are retainable in spite of radical differences in the grammatical forms which are used in the telling of a referential event. In the previous article we gave a sample of how the referential structure can be symbolized for levels of observer relationships. In that article, Figure 1 gave the general usage of the four cells in the notations. Figures 2 and 4 showed differences of observer viewpoint affecting the representation of a single referential event. If we were to repeat the same kind of analysis here, three separate representations would be needed: one for each of the participants in the action—i.e., the events as seen by Abe, by Bill, and by Clara. A fourth representation might be added for the viewpoint of the later narrator, who integrates the actions, feelings, and backgrounds of all three into his telling of the story. In addition, Figure 7 of the preceding article gave formulas for representing persons—from the narrator's viewpoint and the participants' viewpoint.

I will not give extensive referential formulas for the story in this article, since the preceding article is sufficient to give the reader a general sense of the technique. However, a few comments may be helpful. (For details in the analysis of a folktale, see Pike and Pike 1977:365-77; and Howland, in press.)

Class referential cells at different hierarchical levels: At the top of the hierarchy, all versions of the story comprise a single paraphrase set for the story as a whole. Lower levels of the hierarchy involve smaller units—for instance, person. One paraphrase set includes the name *Bill*, referring to this particular Bill in the story, *his* [Abe's] *friend Bill, the one whom she* [Clara] *detested,* [a part of] *they, the one lunching with Abe,* and [the one who] *had met Abe and joined him for lunch.*

Role referential cells at various hierarchical levels: At the top of the hierarchy is the narrator's level. We are told (by me, as creator-"observer" of the narrator) that the narrator delighted in gossiping about the misfortune of others. This characteristic identifies the role of the narration as "gossip," and at the same time (on a lower level—person) identifies one role of the narrator as a person in the community. Bill had a dual role on the person level: he was a friend from Abe's perspective, and a villain (more or less repugnant, at least) from Clara's. Evaluation, purpose, cause and the like are involved in this cell.

Slot referential cells: At the top of the hierarchy, the reported incident fits into the biographies of each of the three participants. At the lower person level, Bill fits into a friendship group which includes Abe but not Clara. Nuclearity of one subevent to another is specified in this cell: the nucleus (or climax) of this story is the interaction between Bill, Abe, and Clara when they meet. No data is included in the story which helps to determine the nuclearity of Abe versus Bill in their friendship. Items or characteristics often remain unknown or ambiguous to the analyst, and the cell affected remains empty or incompletely filled when this is the case.

Cohesion referential cells: In this cell we register the obligatory or optional occurrence of an item, its acceptability in a situation, and its coherence with a larger situation. We specify in these cells factors of background situations, background beliefs, implicit assumptions, attitudes, and truth-versus-falsehood. Each of these serve in some way to determine or control the occurrence of an event, in addition to determining the characteristics of a person or thing which exercises control over events. At the person level in this story, Clara's detestation of Bill is a controlling factor leading to her refusal to eat with the pair and is crucial to the nucleus of the story's plot. In other words, the control originates low in the referential hierarchy, at the level of person, but affects a unit high in that hierarchy, at the level of event. Minor controls leading to the event include the respective needs for going to work (Abe), performing errands (Bill), and going shopping (Clara).

The cohesion cell is also used to indicate truth and falsehood. A "true statement" is cohesive with the general background knowledge of the person doing the evaluating—normally the observer reporting an event. For example, the reporter of our story speaks of Clara's *flimsy excuse*—i.e., her statement was not cohesive with the facts. Cohesion may also be related to social expectancies. Thus, *Oh, I'm feeling fine* may not reflect the details of physiology well known to the hearer; but it is not intended to deceive. In this story we do not have enough information to know whether or not Clara knew that both Abe and Bill were aware that her "illness" was an excuse.

Deliberate negative cohesion can be exploited not only in social excuses, but in humor. Irony often states the opposite of the truth, but without intent to deceive. Similarly, negative cohesion can include misstatement of facts due to ignorance on the part of the speaker. Role is relevant to the understanding of such a situation: the role of deceitful purpose must be present with negative cohesion before lying is encountered.

Figure 10 is a sample four-celled, low-level formula, suggesting Bill's relation to the story; Figure 11 suggests Clara's higher-level event vector.

The preceding paragraphs, combined with the models in the second article, suggest a notation for the referential hierarchy of this story. This notation is sufficient for all of the story variants, except for Figure 9 where an "outside" gossiping observer has been added to the reporting style and needs to be indicated in an appropriate level of notation. In this article the grammatical (telling) order changed radically with each variant of the story. What we have not shown in any of the articles is the four-celled notation for these grammatical differences.

Tagmemics, Discourse, and Verbal Art

SLOT	CLASS
Member of friendship group, with Abe (but marginal, in view of observer, to Clara)	Bill, Abe's friend, he, him, the man Clara detested, the one who ate lunch with Bill, his friend
	Bill, one of the two men eating together, one of the people referred to as "they"
ROLE	COHESION
a) From Abe's view, a friend	Background of intersecting but not identical friendship circles
b) From Clara's perspective, the villain (more or less)	Background of history of relationships with Abe and Clara

Figure 10. **Suggestive Four-Cell Low-Level Tagmeme Formula** to show some of the characteristics of Bill. Note that there may be synonyms for Bill—a paraphrase set—but only this one person is represented in the class (versus an indeterminate number of potentially named persons or objects in a grammatical class for a noun phrase). *Bill* here is not the name of each of a large number of people so labelled, but an entry of this one individual, under whatever name. Referential structure is here, thus, more like an encyclopedia than like a dictionary. The persons involved here are members of a specific cast of characters—not mere names.

Marginal to theme	Clara goes to town	Marginal	She shops	Nuclear to story	Rejects, by excuse invitation to lunch
In order to shop	Needs some items; believes them to be available there	To meet needs (or random interest?)	Enjoys shopping (or must do so?)	In order to avoid time with Bill	Detests Bill Overrides friendship with Abe Belief that lame "excuse" is appropriate

Figure 11. **Suggestive Formula** to show three tagmemes of one vector of the events in the story from the perspective of Clara. Different formulas would be needed for perspectives and experiences of Abe and Bill. A breakdown formula composed of a sequence of included tagmemes would be needed for the third tagmeme, to give fuller detail of the rejection: her glancing up to see them; the invitation by Abe; the refusal by means of an excuse. In the cohesion cell we have Clara's evaluation of (or attitude toward) Bill. We do not know his evaluations of her and so we would have a gap in the comparable tagmeme describing Bill. His purposes and role would also differ.

One alternative for notating the grammar is to use a branching tree diagram for the whole text, related to the sentence diagramming used by teachers of English grammar for scores of years. The branches correspond directly with structural (as opposed to semantic) chunks of the text; and the chunks of text correspond with the levels of hierarchy postulated by tagmemic grammatical theory (e.g., morphemes, words, phrases, clauses, sentences, paragraphs, monologues, single speaker-hearer exchange, conversations). Each branch must be labeled—when the data is available—for slot (above the branch) and role (below it), with the node at the bottom of a branch being labelled for class and cohesion. Finally, sets of comparable tree diagrams for individual texts are combined into general tagmemic formulas which are generative for any text where they are appropriate.

To make tree diagrams and formulas for each level of each story variant is a very large task and cannot be handled within an appropriate space here. (An eleven-sentence story, with just one variant of the telling, covers many pages and charts in Pike and Pike 1977:12-18, 412-54—a contribution made largely by Evelyn Pike, as was the referential treatment of the events of the folktale already referred to, 364-78). But we will provide a sample.

The grammatical outline of the story as told to match Figure 2 is relatively simple. At the top is the story as a whole, followed by three paragraphs describing separately the (simultaneous) experiences of Abe, Bill, and Clara. Change between the paragraphs is known not only by the change of content (referential meaning) but also by the marker *meanwhile,* indicating a shift to the second paragraph, and *also* marking the third paragraph. Changes in the verb phrases (*had left, had gone*) in the last two paragraphs show the "backing up" in time to "restart" the telling so as to represent event-simultaneity. The grammatical arrangement is quite straightforward. See Figure 12 for a branching diagram with each node labelled by a four-cell tagmeme formula.

The grammatical tree structure for each of the tellings would be different in spite of the fact that only one referential structure is present. The tree for the telling illustrated by Figure 4, for example, would have just one paragraph, but the sentence breakdown would be much more complex. The first of these sentences has a complex subject: *Abe, Bill, and Clara* (*had all gone downtown*). The second and third sentences begin with a dependent clause followed by an independent clause (*While Abe and Bill were eating, Clara wandered past,* and *Although invited to join them, she refused*). The tree for the telling illustrated by Figure 8, on the other hand, would be more complex and is beyond the scope of this paper. Many pages would be

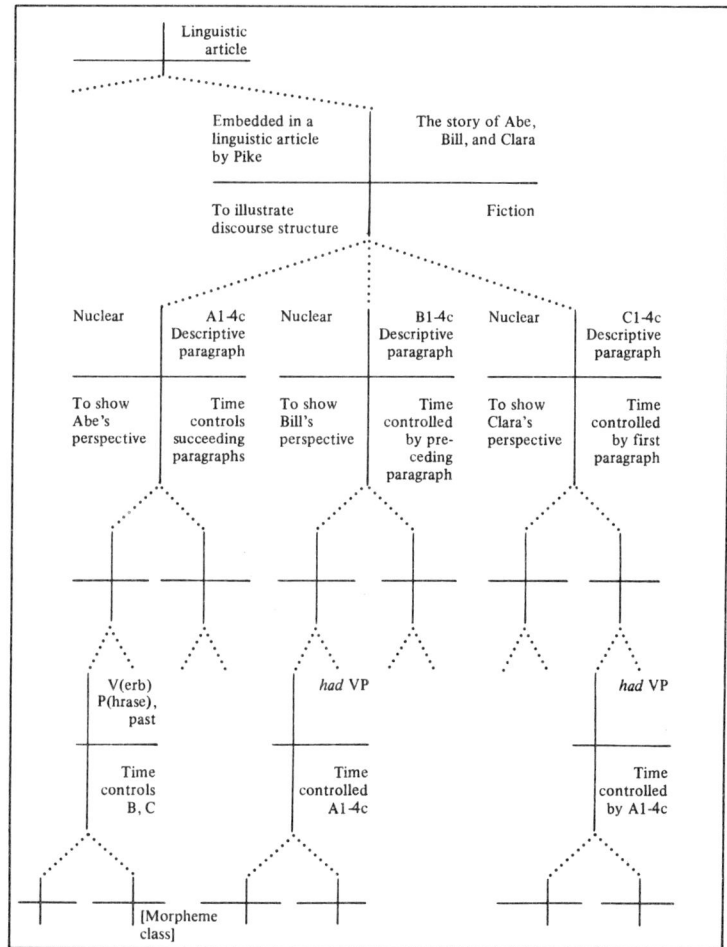

Figure 12. Hints toward the development of a **Branching Diagram** representing the data of Figure 2. At the juncture of each node (at each point where a branch splits into two or more branches) there is a four-cell tagmeme representation by slot, class, role, and cohesion. The slot will meet the need of theories which wish in such diagrams to show things like subject or predicate; the class, those theories which wish to represent only items like noun phrase or verb phrase; the role, those theories which wish to represent only items like actor or goal. But, here, all three (plus cohesion) are given at each level of the hierarchy. In this instance, only the branches into paragraphs is given, plus a lower-level hint about verb phrases. The end of the tree would find morpheme classes represented (e.g., type of verb root, or type of suffix).

needed to analyze the structural relationships of the sentences to each other, to the story as a whole, and to their constituents. Note the need to have an introduction for Figure 3, giving the observer viewpoint (*What an awkward coincidence that was!*), the embedded clauses, phrases, and participles of various types.

When all of the individual diagrams have been made, along with diagrams of different stories, texts, descriptions, sets of instructions, and other sources, the analyst pulls together similar items into four-cell tagmemic formulas which are generalizations applicable to all the data (as opposed to the individual trees which represent single items). These generalizations allow the prediction of specific sentences (or other items) which might be encountered and which would be considered correctly formed within the limits of the grammatical rules involved. Again, it is important to note that grammatical correctness is distinct from referential correctness. Truth and error do not have a place in the grammatical hierarchy. In order to illustrate one of these formulas we will use a simple, active declarative transitive clause root (i.e., a clause with subject-predicate-object, but without time, means, or other such modification). Figure 13 is a list of clauses from the story in its various tellings; below this list the formula itself is given in four-celled form and applies to each clause.

The top of the list includes simple clauses like *He met Abe* (from Figure 1.B2), where a single pronoun fills the subject slot. On the other hand, the coordination of the two personal nouns—*Abe and Bill*—fills the same slot in Figure 9.AB2-3. The set of objects (labelled "adjunct as undergoer" in Pike and Pike 1977) is more complicated. The objects include a single pronoun (e.g., *her*), an unmodified personal name (*Bill*), a demonstrative (*this*), a count-noun phrase (*a flimsy excuse*), an infinitive clause (*her to join them*), and a comparable infinitive structure without the pronoun (*to lunch together*). The predicate is a simple verb in past tense (e.g., *met*), except for the phrase in pluperfect (*had met*); I have treated *made-up* (Figure 8.C4c) as a special verb phrase.

Numerous items have been omitted from this tagmeme formula: the time item *just*; the clause marker *of course*; and the post-object subject appositional elements *myself* and *simply*. Because these are omitted we are dealing with *clause roots*; if they were included we would be dealing with *clauses*. In addition, I have omitted *she refused* (Figure 4.C4) since I consider it to be off-norm. The object of *she refused*—"to join them"—is implicit since it occurred in the preceding clause of the same sentence (*Although invited to join them, she refused*) and serves for the two predicates in dual function. (For dual role of subject, see Pike and Pike 1977:354, 357-58). I have also

Figure 1.A2 . . . . He . . . . met . . . . Bill.
and Figure 5.A
Figure 1.B2 . . . . He . . . . met . . . . Abe.
Figure 1.C4c . . . She . . . . did . . . . this.
Figure 9.C4c . . . Clara . . . . cut . . . . Bill.
Figure 7.C4c . . . Clara . . . . made-up . . . . . . a flimsy excuse.
Figure 7.C4c . . . She . . . . made-up . . . . . . a flimsy excuse.
Figure 1.C4b . . . They . . . . invited . . . . . . her to join them.
Figure 1.A4b . . . (But even though) Abe . . . invited . . . . her.
Figure 9.0 . . . . . I . . . (just) . . . . heard . . . . it (myself).
Figure 9.AB2-3 . . (Of course) you . . . . realize . . . . . . that both Abe and
Bill had met and . . .
Figure 9.AB2-3 . . Abe and Bill . . . . had started . . . . to lunch together.
Figure 7.C4c . . . She (simply) . . . . refused . . . . to eat with Bill.

Normal Active Declarative Clause Root =

SLOT Subject -	CLASS(ES) -Personal noun or noun phrase, simple or compound -Pronoun	SLOT Predicate -	CLASS(ES) -Verb or verb phrase, simple, or verb with adverb	SLOT Object - (Adjunct)	CLASS(ES) -Personal noun -Count noun phrase -Pronoun -Infinitive clause or phrase
+		+		+	
ROLE Actor -	COHESION -Controls agreement of verb phrase in number; and some semantic control -Obligatory	ROLE Statement -	COHESION -Transitive -Controls occurrence of object -Number controlled by subject -Some mutual semantic control with subject and object -Obligatory present as mutually controlling nor- mal presence of subject and object -Tense con- trolled from position in chronological sequence plus place in telling	ROLE Undergoer - (goal, patient)	COHESION -Presence normally obligatory, mutually controlled by transi- tive verb phrase

Figure 13. Normal Active Declarative Transitive Clause Roots, as occurring in the tellings of the story about Abe, Bill, and Clara, are charted here in columns for subject, predicate, and object. Below the columns are the respective tagmemes for those elements, *generalizing* on the illustrations above. Omitted are passive or interrogative or imperative types, temporal modifications of the clause, conjunctions, and special occurrences where the context of the telling allows the object to be omitted (so that the object shows up *in the norm*, as given in the formula, as obligatory). This kind of notation systematically provides more information—and hence is much more complex—than the formula which gives *only* the slot (e.g., subject), *or* class (e.g., noun), *or* role (e.g., actor); and it requires more data than one which does not include reference to agreement in time, number, or semantics.

omitted, as off-norm, the count noun *Boy* used without modifiers in *Boy meets girl* (Figure 9.0); *they met* (Figure 7.A4); and *They ate together* (Figure 5.A3).

Before we would be able to symbolize fully a transitive clause, these omitted items (and others from other texts) would have to be included in amplified or related formulas: for example, passives (which do not occur here); imperatives (Figure 9.C4a *Believe it or not—oh boy, what a situation!*); interrogatives (Figure 3.A4b *What could they do?*); and exclamatory items (Figure 9.0 *Would you ever believe it!*, and Figure 9.0 *Life does have its amusing coincidences*). It would take a full grammar of English to handle these structures and others at all levels and in all their contrasts and variants. What is presented here is only a hint as to the direction in which such an analysis might go.

III. CONCLUSION

Until recently, most linguists in the United States have confined their attention to sentences and their included parts. Gradually they are extending their analyses to larger units—paragraphs, monologues, and conversations. With this new focus, linguists may hope to integrate their work with that of literary scholars. This article has explored one facet of literature which contributes to its power or weakness, success or failure: the structure of telling. In telling one story many different ways—to change the focus, or highlight emotional or content concerns—we were forced to use different grammatical structures, some of which were more complex than others. This organized study of variations in the grammatical and referential hierarchies has interesting implications for instructors of composition. Students who need to be taught to form complex sentences may benefit from an exercise which requires them to restructure a story, since some telling orders *elicit* complex sentences.

The second part of this article has shown how tagmemic formulas can represent the kinds of clause data familiar to all of us. The advantage of tagmemic formulas is that they capture the complexity of the data in a single approach. Tagmemic formulas are also capable of representing off-norm forms, and these formulas may help beginning students to see clearly the large range of options available to them in telling and writing: alternatives in context, presentation, and perspective. But if tagmemic formulas can help students learning to write expository prose in English, we regard that outcome as an incidental but appropriate outcome of the very different purpose for which they were developed: to provide a generally useful scheme for studying the structures of the languages of the world. Most people think that the order in which things are told in their own language is the most natural and logical one, but when we study other languages (especially, from our point of view, ones far removed from "Standard Average European"), we find that *natural* and *logical* depend upon the viewpoint of the observer. In Irian Jay on the western part of the island of New Guinea, for example, Westrum (1976) spent a year learning the Berik language and found no words that would translate the English words *if, while, but, because, since* or *therefore*. In Berik, such relations are expressed in the sequence of telling. If a speaker of Berik says, "John ate poison; he died," he means both *John died after he ate the poison* and *John died because he ate the poison*; the sequence of telling conveys the relations expressed in the English words *after* and *because*. The Berik speaker sees no need for these words, nor can he imagine any reason to tell about these events outside their "natural" order of happening. Tagmemics provides a useful set of techniques that enable observers to discover the relations between grammar and reference in any given language, however far removed from their own. By recognizing that "natural" orders and sequences are conditioned by our language, we can better appreciate the constraints (and the opportunities) that a given language imposes upon its speakers.

Bibliography

Becker, Judith O., and Alton L. Becker. "A Musical Icon: Power and Meaning in Javanese Gamelon Music." In *The Sign in Music and Literature.* Ed. Wendy L. Steiner. Austin: University of Texas Press, 1981.

Blacking, John. "The Problems of 'Ethnic' Perceptions in the Semiotics of Music." In *The Sign in Music and Literature.* Ed. Wendy L. Steiner. Austin: University of Texas Press, 1981.

Blake, William. "The Sick Rose." *The Poetry and Prose of William Blake.* Ed. David V. Erdman. Garden City: Doubleday, 1968.

Chatman, Seymour. "How Do We Establish New Codes of Verisimilitude?" In *The Sign in Music and Literature.* Ed. Wendy L. Steiner. Austin: University of Texas Press, 1981.

Ciardi, John. *How Does a Poem Mean?* Boston: Houghton Mifflin Co., 1959.

Erickson, Carol J., and Evelyn G. Pike. "Semantic and Grammatical Structures of an Isirawa Narrative." In *From Baudi to Indonesian.* Ed. Ignatius Suharno, and Kenneth L. Pike. Irian Jaya: Cenderawasih University and Summer Institute of Linguistics, 1976, 63-93.

Gordon, David, and George Lakoff. "Conversation Postulates." In *Papers from the Seventh Regional Meeting of the Chicago Linguistic Society.* Chicago: Chicago Linguistic Society, 1971, 63-84.

Grice, H. Paul. "Logic and Conversation." In *Speech Acts.* (From William James Lectures, Harvard, 1967). Ed. Peter Cole and Jerry L. Morgan. Vol. 3. New York: Academic Press, 1975, 41-58.

Grimes, Joseph E. "Outlines and Overlays." *Language,* 48 (1972), 513-24.

―――*The Thread of Discourse.* The Hague: Mouton, 1975.

――― ed. *Papers on Discourse.* Arlington, Texas: Summer Institute of Linguistics Publications in Linguistics and Related Fields 51, 1978.

Howland, Lilian G. "Communicational Integration of Reality and Fiction." *Language and Communication,* 1 (1981), 89-148.

Hrushovski, Benjamin. "The Structure of Semiotic Objects: A Three-Dimensional Model." In *The Sign in Music and Literature.* Ed. Wendy L. Steiner. Austin: University of Texas Press, 1981.

Jones, Linda Kay. *Theme in English Expository Discourse.* Lake Bluff, Ill.: Jupiter Press, 1977.

Keiler, Allan R. "Two Views of Musical Semiotics." In *The Sign in Music and Literature.* Ed. Wendy L. Steiner. Austin: University of Texas Press, 1981.

Larson, Mildred L. *The Functions of Reported Speech in Discourse.* Diss.: The University of Texas at Arlington, 1977.

Lewis, C.S. *Surprised by Joy: The Shape of My Early Life.* New York: Harcourt, Brace and World, 1955.

Longacre, Robert E. *Discourse, Paragraph, and Sentence Structure in Selected Philippine Languages.* Santa Ana, California: Summer Institute of Linguistics, Publications in Linguistics and Related Fields 21, [1968-69] 1970.

Martin, Howard R., and Kenneth L. Pike. "An Analysis of the Vocal Performance of a Poem: A Classification of Intonational Features." *Language and Style,* 7 (1974), 209-18.

Perlman, Alan, and Daniel L. Greenblatt. "Miles Davis Meets Noam Chomsky: Some Observations on Jazz Improvisation and Language Structure." In *The Sign in Music and Literature.* Ed. Wendy L. Steiner. Austin: University of Texas Press, 1981.

Pike, Kenneth L. *The Intonation of American English.* Ann Arbor: University of Michigan Press, 1945.

——— *Language in Relation to a Unified Theory of the Structure of Human Behavior.* 2nd ed. The Hague: Mouton, 1967. [First edition 1954, 1955, 1960].

———"Implications of the Patterning of an Oral Reading of a Set of Poems." *Poetics,* 1 (1971a), 38-45.

———*Mark My Words.* Grand Rapids, MI: Erdman's, 1971b.

———"Toward the Development of Tagmemic Postulates." In *Tagmemics.* Ed. Kenneth L. Pike and Ruth M. Brend. Vol. II. The Hague: Mouton; 1976, 91-127.

———"Grammatical versus Referential Hierarchies." *The Third LACUS Forum* (1977a), 345-55.

——— ed. *Pilot Projects on the Reading of English of Science and Technology.* Ann Arbor: University of Michigan Papers in Linguistics, Special Publications in Applied Linguistics 1, 1977.

——— and Evelyn G. Pike. *Grammatical Analysis*. Dallas: Summer Institute of Linguistics Publications in Linguistics 53, 1977.

——— and Stephen B. Pike. *Songs of Fun and Faith*. Lake Bluff, Ill.: Jupiter Press, 1977.

Richards, I.A. *Practical Criticism: A Study of Literary Judgment* [1929]. New York: Harcourt-Brace, 1956.

Ruwet, Nicolas. "Typography, Rhyme, and Linguistic Structures in Poetry." In *The Sign in Music and Literature*. Ed. Wendy L. Steiner. Austin: University of Texas Press, 1981.

Searle, John R. "What is a Speech Act?" In *Language and Social Context*. Ed. Pier Paolo Giglioli. Baltimore: Penguin, 1972, pp. 136-54.

Sebeok, Thomas A. "Prefigurements of Art: Animal Architecture." *Image and Code*. Ed. Wendy L. Steiner. Ann Arbor, Mich.: Michigan Studies in the Humanities, 1981, 43-56.

Westrum, Susan. "Chronological Mapping as a Useful Tool in Identifying Semantic Groupings in Berik, Irian Jaya, Indonesia." In *From Baudi to Indonesian*. Ed. Ignatius Suharno, and Kenneth L. Pike. Irian Jaya: Cenderawasih University and Summer Institute of Linguistics, 1976, 63-93.

Wise, Mary Ruth. *Identification of Participants in Discourse: A Study of Aspects of Form and Meaning in Nomatsiquenga*. Norman, Oklahoma: Summer Institute of Linguistics Publications in Linguistics and Related Fields 28, 1971.

Young, Richard, Alton Becker, and Kenneth L. Pike. *Rhetoric: Discovery and Change*. New York: Harcourt, 1970.